The Transformation of a DOUBTING THOMAS

Growing from a Cynic to a Professional in the Corporate World

Thomas B. Dowd III

Copyright ©2012 Thomas B. Dowd III

ISBN: 978-1-938883-06-4

All rights reserved. No part of this book may be reproduced or transmitted in any form or by any means, electronic or mechanical, including photocopying, recording, or by any information storage and retrieval system, without permission in writing from the author.

Designed and produced by
Maine Authors Publishing
558 Main Street
Rockland, Maine 04841
www.maineauthorspublishing.com

Printed in the United States of America

Note: The views expressed are my own and not those of my current or former employers.
—Thomas B. Dowd III

*Dedicated to my three beautiful daughters
Meg, Erin, and Tatum,
and my incredible wife Ellen,
who have taught me personal lessons I have been
able to carry into my professional life.
Thank you for your patience and
for being an active part of my learning process.*

Contents

PART I— Vision and Mission
   Vision and Mission 3
   Introduction: The Roots of My Transformation 4

Part II The Transformation
1. Get a Mentor 17
2. Be a Mentor, and Learn Something Yourself. 20
3. Have Unprofessional Days—Gain Trust and Respect 22
4. Dedicate Time Daily, Weekly, and Monthly to Writing Down Your Accomplishments—What Went Right? 24
5. Stop and Smell the Roses—or At Least Stop and Say Hi 26
6. Send a Note to Say Thank You, and Mean It 28
7. Learn to Communicate Assertively 30
8. Understand that Winning Isn't Everything—Losing Is 33
9. Wait Three Months....................................... 36
10. Stand Up for What's Right............................... 38
11. Differentiate Yourself—Make It Known 41
12. Be Impatiently Patient 44
13. Prove People Wrong.................................... 47
14. Prove People Right 50
15. Have Multiple and Diverse Role Models.................. 53
16. Write Down Your Goals…in Pencil 57
17. Control What You Can Control (You Have More Control Than You Think)................ 59
18. Show Compassion 62
19. Set an Example 64
20. Do Something With Book Recommendations.............. 66
21. Live in the Present 69
22. Work Smarter, Not Harder 72
23. Let Your Music Out 75
24. Open the Gift of Feedback.............................. 78
25. Step Away and Clear Your Head........................ 81
26. Be Aware That "Nobody is Not Trying".................. 83
27. Don't Let People Leave Their Manager, or the Company 87
28. Be Flexible and Adaptable.............................. 90
29. Have the Right Priorities and Set the Right Perspective 93
30. Build a Network 95
31. Lead the Parade.. 99
32. Be Sensitive to Multiple Generations in the Workplace 102
33. Control Self-imposed Pressures 106
34. Play Music in the Background 109

35. Do You Know Your Value Proposition?.................. 111
36. Build Credibility and Success
    through Effective Communication 113
37. Understand Communication Preferences................ 118
38. Know What the Written Word Says About You 120
39. Learn the Value of Effective Verbal Communication 124
40. Take Action—Hope Won't Win the Game
    without a Game Plan 127
41. Learn to Manage Up, Down, and Around................ 130
42. Laugh at Work; Laugh With Others.................... 135
43. Build and Maintain a Strong Résumé 138
44. Manage Your Time, Don't Let it Manage You—Part I 142
45. Manage Your Time, Don't Let it Manage You—Part II 146
46. Manage Your Time, Don't Let it Manage You—Part III..... 148
47. Don't Try to Boil the Ocean......................... 152
48. Be Responsible With the Power of Position (P.O.P.) 154
49. Know When to Let Go and Move On (Get Over It)........ 157
50. Send Your Message to One Person and Watch it Grow 160
51. Become a Good Listener 162
52. Be the Bigger Person 164
53. Surround Yourself With Pictures 166
54. Get to Know the People You Work With................ 168
55. Balance Being a Leader and a Doer—
    You Can't Do Both at the Same Time................... 170
56. Give People Second Chances 172
57. Do Stuff You Love.................................. 175
58. Share Best Practices 178
59. Take Time for Yourself—You Deserve It 180
60. Get Involved at Work, at School, or at Life
    and Find Out How Contagious It Is................... 182
61. Know the Whole Story.............................. 185
62. Be Yourself—the Paradox 187
63. Treat Each Day Like an Interview—Another Paradox 190
64. Be a Teacher—You Will Learn More 193
65. Value People 195
66. Revisit the Things That Made You Better and Stronger..... 197

Part III Conclusion
What Now?.. 200
References 206
Acknowledgements...................................... 208
About the Author 210

PART I
Vision and Mission

Vision and Mission

My vision for writing this book is to provide a simple-to-follow, written guide for professionals hoping to develop their skills in a multitude of areas including communication, leadership, organization, and networking. The lessons are based on my own professional experiences over more than twenty years in a corporate environment. I want to utilize my experiences gained from work, my membership in Toastmasters International (a group of 270,000 world-wide members looking to improve their communication and leadership skills) and the National Speakers Association, and from the epiphanies I have experienced by teaching a professional development series. In addition to my normal job responsibilities, I started investing time with emerging leaders and experienced managers a couple years ago in an attempt to teach my lessons to others. I want to spread those teachings to a broader audience.

My mission is to create an easy-to-read guide that will motivate and inspire you to take the steps to transform yourself. I want you to improve your professional experiences and increase the positive impacts you have on the people around you. Whether you are working in a small business or a large corporation, you will be able to apply these examples and teachings to your situation. Whether you are a manager, an entry-level employee just joining a company, someone struggling to get through the daily grind, or a professional striving to reach the heights of your career, there will be something in here for you. This book will navigate through key teaching moments from my professional life and offer you a simple reference guide for better organizing your professional life and effectively maneuvering through the complexities of communication, relationship building, and organization.

Introduction

The Roots of My Transformation

My transformation has put me on top of the world. Even in the midst of "The Great Recession," and working for one of the larger financial institutions in the world, I have never been as happy as I am right now with my professional success, my performance, my positive influence on others around me, and my confidence in my ability to make a difference in the corporate environment. It has not always been that way.

I was previously an executive employed with Bank of America, prior to changing companies. I was with MBNA, before the Bank of America merger. My former company had to go through a significant economic downturn starting in 2008 like all of us, while going through intense company media and government scrutiny, which added to employee pressures. None of these challenges were as great as my personal challenge to grow within the company, and to look inward to realize I had control of my own success. As you will see, I have had extensive roadblocks that could have negatively influenced my next steps and overall career. I had to do some soul searching in order to determine if I wanted to remain with the company, let alone to develop and mature with it. Through it all, I was determined to find a way to make a difference as a leader.

I am stronger than ever. I have missed plenty of my self-established professional goals over my twenty-plus years of employment. However, I have never been more satisfied with my personal growth, my professional capabilities, and my passion for the people I proudly call co-workers, and that satisfaction has nothing to do with compensation (although good compensation doesn't hurt). I have found constant satisfaction with my newfound effort and positive attitude, even on so-called bad days. I did not wake up one morning and say, "Today is the day I am going to be happy." I did, however, start to add up certain milestones in my career and compare them to my previous professional goals and timelines. I realized that I needed to take a more active role if I wanted to thrive, not just survive, in my day-to-day professional life. I also came to the realization that I could have a great positive impact on the business and the people around me. In return, my own satisfaction level skyrocketed as I transformed. I had to take accountability if I wanted to make the difference I knew I could.

Although I have worked hard and always considered myself a loyal employee, I have not always been happy. My satisfaction level influenced how I acted and how I was perceived. I was often characterized as having cynical and defensive behaviors. Many thought I had a bad attitude in my professional life. I didn't believe anything was my fault, including my limited promotions, slow growth, and inconsistent satisfaction level. I am not exactly sure where these personality traits came from. I know through long-term self-awareness and a couple of personality tests, that I am an introverted person who is driven to succeed. Maybe these cynical postures were my personal way to defend against any lack of success or roadblocks. I had a natural excuse built in because it was never my fault. I used my defensive reactions as a protective mechanism to compensate for my shyness and physical reactions.

As an introverted individual, I was not ready for the corporate world. I constantly broke out in hives and blushed when facing tense moments—and my definition of tense was broad. My whole body shook when I had to interact with someone. I would be quick with an answer in order to make the question go away, or I would make a curt comment so I would be done with the interaction quickly. Being such a shy and withdrawn individual kept me from effectively initiating conversations. I could not maintain and sustain personal and professional dialogues in which I could get to know people, and they could get to know me. As a result, I was labeled professionally as one of the following: unapproachable, stuck up, or not a "people person." In my eyes, this was not the case. However, my eyes were not making my career decisions, writing my performance appraisals, or creating these inaccurate assessments. I, in turn, took on stances and positions that were terse, to the point, and blunt so that I could move on to my next task and assignment. I liked working independently and seemed to be happiest doing my own thing. The problem was that I did like helping customers and grew to appreciate being in leadership positions.

I used all of the excuses as to why I didn't progress at the speed I thought I should have: A manager didn't like me. I was not given a fair shot. The other person must have an inside track or must be related to a senior leader. I blamed everyone and everything. My managers must be reading my past reviews and refusing to see my growth. They couldn't

The Transformation of a Doubting Thomas

push beyond their old perceptions and see my improvement. I had changed and nobody saw it. I found out over time, I was not changing or evolving—at least not at any perceptible pace—and everyone but me saw it. I lacked the ability to adapt, at least at the speed of business.

Don't get me wrong. I did advance in my career—more a product of my refusal to fail than an ability to mature into a leader. I was in a variety of roles that included call centers, customer service, management, administration, project management, risk mitigation, and business governance. In a career spanning over twenty years, I now realize that I was in an enviable position that many people would crave. I had variety. I had support from many people I worked with, who had the ability to look past my stubbornness and did not give up on me. They gave me the feedback I didn't want to hear.

I had the drive to succeed, but first I had a lot to learn about myself. I am not talking about the technical aspects of a job. With a Bachelor of Arts, I was trained in being flexible to learn in different ways about many things. I have never really been concerned about losing my job, at least on a day-to-day basis. I have always worked hard and the job always got done, even if it meant pushing the people who worked for me too hard. Other times, I tried to do everything on my own and refused assistance.

I've had some obvious signs over the years that there were different ways to go about my business. First, after earning my first manager role within my first three years at the company, my title of manager was removed after only one year on the job. I was devastated, especially since it was my first legitimate leadership position. I reasoned that it must have been because I never had a day off, I was managing for three months with no assistance after my peer changed jobs, and I was left with over thirty people to look after. I remember vividly coming home from work and saying to my roommates that I should be paid extra for babysitting. My direct reports gave feedback that I was unapproachable, I had favorites, and I could not drive the business.

Remember, nothing was my fault. My computer system was toward the back of my desk; it wasn't my fault that I looked busy when someone approached from behind. How was I supposed to know they were even there? There were a couple of people who had interests similar to mine, including sports teams. I enjoyed talking to these people more than others. Of course, I would still answer everyone's questions. The company and business were going through so many changes. My boss sat at his desk and never gave me feedback. How could I drive the business with no direction from my manager? I had to get my feedback from focus groups and the rumor mill. The excuses piled up. Still, it couldn't be true, could it?

The Roots of My Transformation

I was given a position in computer programming. I disliked my job. I hated staring at a computer all day with limited interaction with my co-workers. Even though I had been "babysitting," I had begun to tolerate the interactions enough to miss them. I was an Interpersonal and Organizational Communication major in college. I knew nothing about programming, and I could never get used to sitting in a silent room with people who would rather click away at the keys of a computer than talk to me. It was a lonely position to be in. It was also my first glimpse at self-awareness and my need to change.

The next six months had me peering from the outside looking in. I felt eerily like the character Scrooge looking in at my Christmas past and future at the same time. My old team was in a room next to me, and I watched the new manager run that team. Under the new manager, they were happier, performing better, the business was running smoothly, and I didn't seem to be missed. The long-term lessons still had quite some time before they would take hold, but the seed was planted. I look back at this time in my career as a milestone.

A change was needed. I had heard that there was a position open in a new Maine office. I was in the Delaware office, where I had been for my first five years. I saw those five years starting to slip away if I didn't do something differently. I was miserable. I approached the executive who oversaw the entire business and said that I wanted another shot at managing. I asked if he would consider me. He said (paraphrased), "I don't see you in a senior manager role in the next five years, so I don't want you managing. You're free to accept another position in an administrative role to support the business. However, you need to speak to the new manager first for his final decision."

I approached my potential new manager, who was familiar with my work and background. The first thing he said was something along the lines of, "Do you realize that you are cynical and that that is not healthy for a newly emerging business?" I had heard the term "cynical" many times in my life. However, I had never been labeled cynical. I had a reputation that was now coming to light. First, I was given direct feedback that I apparently needed, badly. Second, I left the meeting with the need to look up the word. I had an idea what it meant, but I needed to put it into context to gain a true understanding of how it related to me. According to dictionary.com, it "suggests a disbelief in the sincerity of human motives." Ouch! I still had the drive to succeed. I was motivated more than ever. I wasn't going to let anyone or anything cause me to fail. I was also still fuming over the comment from the first manager, who had said he couldn't see me in a senior manager role.

The Transformation of a Doubting Thomas

I didn't like being told that I couldn't do or be something. I left the office and prepared my reasons for why I would be able to make a difference with the new business in Maine. The follow-up meeting was a success… kind of. I could go to Maine in a business support position, and potentially earn my way into a manager position. Managing people was not a right, it was a privilege. I had to earn it again.

I took on the business support role with fervor, determined to prove everyone wrong and that I belonged in a leadership role. I unknowingly ended up becoming a special part of a start-up business. The administrative aspects of the job would also teach me valuable skills in organization, teamwork, partnerships, and building bridges that ended up making me a more effective leader…eventually.

Over time, I did get back into managing people and vowed (kind of) to never return to my first managerial ways. Old habits are hard to break, however; it is often referred to as "muscle memory." I meandered through many managerial positions. I did learn from some of my past mistakes. I made the effort to speak to more people and drive my business forward.

I was able to push the right buttons—"push" being the operative word. I pushed people hard to achieve the numbers, thus pushing them away. I negatively impacted the people who worked for me even though our goals were being achieved. I was once asked the question, "If you ran through a wall, would people follow?" If they did follow, did they do it because they knew I could take them where they wanted to be and did they believe in my leadership? Or, did they follow me out of fear, or a feeling of obligation to the business? If I ran through a wall, people might have followed—but not for the right reasons.

I didn't care what they thought of me. I cared about my results. I thought that was what all my managers wanted: results. Cold, hard numbers. I always achieved the expected numbers, but I couldn't understand why I would get poor feedback relating to my style. I was a communication major in college; I did not understand why my communication style was under constant scrutiny. It took me many more years to learn that I could get even better results by caring for people. I revisited the question often as I truly looked toward my transformation: "If you ran through a wall, would people follow?" I knew what the answer *should* be; I just had not acted in a way that made people want to follow me.

I am not sure how, but I was finally promoted to a position in which I would manage other managers. This was a position I had longed for and thought I deserved much earlier in my career. As you can tell from the last statement, defensive people have difficulty letting go—it couldn't have been my fault.

The Roots of My Transformation

Part of the prestige of the position was having my first office with a door. I think subconsciously I was probably happy that I could shut the world out and finally get some work done. I still knew I needed to do some self-reflection, because my work was to motivate people. I was not naïve enough to think I could succeed without changing at least a little bit. I opened the cabinet door in my new office for the first time and saw a sign that read, "Change is inevitable, growth is optional." This became another milestone in my career. There was no author noted—just a simple set of six words.

There are very few short and simple quotes in life that have hit me as hard as this one. I have changed offices many times in my career and have never moved without this small piece of paper. With that simple quote, I was given a lesson in staying grounded. Everything changes. I had to ask myself, "Was I evolving with the business? Was I adapting to my people's needs? Was I making myself better and stronger each day? When I was in the throes of tough times, was I strong enough to learn and lead?" I began to see the light—a light I would need years later.

In the middle of a summer vacation seven hundred miles away from home, my wife's aunt came across the yard and announced that it was interesting that my company had just been bought. My relaxation instantly vanished, followed by a flood of stress and worry. I had no idea what was going to happen to me or my company. The surprise announcement became another milestone in my career. It was more of an unintended crossroad. I had no desire to leave the company. Besides, this company was all I knew. I'd graduated college on a Friday and started at the company the very next Monday. This company was the culture I had grown to know and love. Even cynical Tom used the word "love" in this case; I loved what I'd invested so much time in. I was given very little information about the buyout. There were even fewer answers to my questions over the last couple of days of vacation, when I spoke to people in the office.

I came back from vacation and began the new journey. I failed to mention here that during this merger announcement, I was starting a new job. It was given to me a week before the announcement. I was told it was a "ninety-day task force" overseeing reporting and incentives. What was once great news now caused great angst when I thought about the new role. Not only was I on a task force, I was in an administrative role that could be seen as duplicative when comparing the two entities. I was confident in my own abilities, but the unknown still frightened me.

The flood of change came quickly. The new personal growth moments came to me fast and furious. There was a lot of work ahead to merge the

The Transformation of a Doubting Thomas

companies together. I was an extremely hard worker with a significant depth of internal business knowledge, so I knew that would be a plus if I used it effectively. However, I was also in a position that could be seen as redundant in some eyes or, alternatively, an asset in other decision makers' eyes. I had choices to make.

I spent years in college as part of my major concentrating my studies on organizational structures and cultures. I learned the impact of significant changes on individuals and companies. I was starting to see the value of my studies in play and knew that I could make a difference with respect to my own acceptance of the new world, and possibly get others on board, too. I saw the positive potential of a fresh start.

I built bridges, learned the company culture, and sold the merits of the new company. I was buying into the new culture earlier than others. The previous culture had been perceived by some as elitist. It should have been. We were great at what we did. However, the "we" was now part of the whole "us" of the company. Cultural integration was necessary to transition effectively. The new company was almost ten times larger than the previous. In fact, an executive mentioned to me that you could virtually hide and go unnoticed in a company of this size. I didn't know how to react. I could go into survival mode and try to hide in the enormity. However, I could also go on a quest to meet the 270,000 other employees, learn about the company culture and mission, and build bridges so we all could win. Working smarter, networking more effectively, and creating my own opportunities was key to my survival.

I started to work with people from the "other" company and found that they were part of the greater whole. As time went on, the leaders who resisted change or forced their own culture on others fell behind. The leaders who merged the best of both worlds thrived. I was starting to like this new company, recognizing that if I performed well, things would take care of themselves. I had a fresh slate of people who couldn't get their hands on my personnel file—both the real file and the fictional one I'd created in my mind based on my perception of others' opinions of me. I had a full runway to prove myself. I learned over time that every day was a clean slate. I just carried baggage with me unnecessarily for far too long.

I joined a local Toastmasters International club. The club was chartered almost a year prior but had never met. For selfish reasons, I saw the personal challenge of getting something new up and running, and had been looking for a way to make a name for myself as a leader. Besides, I thought I could boost my résumé. I no longer had anyone I directly worked with in the local office. In the new company, we were spread all over the country and all over the world, and spent a lot of time on conference calls. Toastmasters provided me with a little extra face-to-face personal interaction that I thirsted for in the newer culture. In a deeper reality, I needed to communicate more effectively if I wanted to move forward with my career. I had no idea how much Toastmasters would change my life and career.

I felt this strange selfless need to teach others around me, and was enjoying the leadership of the position. The boost on my résumé was nice, but not as important as the difference I could make. I had no formal influence over others, so that leadership was coming from the heart. I also felt I was gaining confidence in my own communication style. I wanted to help people around me hone their own communication skills. If I could work with some of them, I could help them tell their stories better, increase their own confidence, and be a small part of their success.

The mission of Toastmasters International is "to provide a mutually supportive and positive learning environment in which every individual member has the opportunity to develop oral communication and leadership skills, which in turn foster self-confidence and personal growth." The fact that the mission caught my attention in such a selfless manner pleasantly surprised me. I think the protective cocoon of a smaller group of individuals all working at their own pace toward the same goals inspired me. It became therapeutic, easing my own anxiety, worry, and stress. It became an outlet to turn my internal and intimate stories into a collective diary of narratives to share with the masses. I was often seen as all business in my demeanor. I used this new communication channel as a potential outlet to allow me to share the personal side and warmth I had not been overtly exhibiting over so many years.

In the past, if I was in a room full of people I barely knew, I would freeze. I typically kept to myself or stayed close to people I knew well. I called this my Cocktail Party Syndrome. With Toastmasters, I was slowly coming out of my shell. I was learning to be myself—and enjoying it. I began to ask more questions of people, which allowed me to engage in the conversation and allowed them to open up to me. I was learning the benefits of two-way communication. People began to know more about me through my speeches, and saw that I was defining my personality. I learned about the personal side of our club members through their speeches.

Toastmasters helped me on the professional side. Although I originally joined just to pad my résumé, I was starting to see what motivated people, interested people, and frustrated people because I was interacting more effectively and communicating with a new confidence. Toastmasters was teaching me to relate.

I gained enough confidence to push my limits. I enjoyed the

The Transformation of a Doubting Thomas

competition of Toastmaster contests. I knew it would improve my ability to prepare for stressful situations, like contests, and push myself further. In the Spring 2010 International Speech Contest, I wrote a very personal speech about my dog. I decided a couple of days before my club competition to put on a hat with a dog face on the front of it. I instantly saw a smile every time I placed it on my head. Besides audience reactions, I had people tell me stories about their own dogs and cats. I was learning more about conversation starters. It was so much more interesting than the weather (living in Maine, I always get the question, "Has it snowed yet?"). More importantly, the people I had worked with for so many years commented that they had never seen me like this—and that was a good thing. I was changing others' perceptions of me simply by being myself.

I was doing something I had once thought was impossible. I previously blamed my managers for their inability to see past the old me, certain that I didn't need to improve my communication skills. I knew somewhere deep down that I was wrong, but did not have the courage to take the actions necessary to change. Toastmasters became my public diary of stories I hadn't realized I wanted or needed to share.

I had been with Toastmasters for about eighteen months and had been involved in multiple contests before I chose to share a speech for the first time with my wife, Ellen. My wife is my confidante, my constant strength, and my shoulder to lean on. Yet, the hesitancy to have her see me so vulnerable frightened me. Now, I think that I didn't want to disappoint her or have her see me trying to push myself beyond my comfort zone. It probably didn't help that I mentioned her in just about every speech I wrote.

She is a wonderful storyteller and an inspiration. Maybe, a small part of me was trying to have her accept me just a little more. My conservative personality held me back until I realized as I progressed further into that particular contest that I needed her. She had always told me she believed in me; I knew she did, but couldn't push myself to do the same. The first time I ever gave the speech to her, I compressed a seven-minute speech into five minutes by talking too quickly. I have never been so nervous, even in front of hundreds of people.

The shortened speech wasn't the only gaffe. There was a particular statistic I typically give about saving the lives of millions of dogs and cats. I was so anxious that I left the letter "s" off the word "cats." Ellen couldn't stop laughing. It was a priceless scene. She wasn't laughing at me—she was just wondering why I only wanted to save the life of one cat. She was telling me that it was all right to make mistakes and laugh at myself. She also was teaching me how important it was to enjoy the moment. She had opened my eyes further. I knew I needed her more than ever. She had always been there offering support and saying, "Just tell me what you want me to do, and I will do it to help you." This was a simple phrase that needed a simple action to prove it. I now turn to her more and more in life, not just for speeches.

I am not a CEO writing my memoir. I am a simple person who has learned simple lessons in life that I want to share. I have learned lessons that probably took far too long for me to grasp. The lessons I want to impart to you may not be complex, but they are valuable. There are times when we need to learn things for ourselves in order to make a truly lasting impression. I want to provide you with some of the most lasting impressions that have come to me through my professional interactions. I want to share the mistakes I've made, and share the common-sense teachings that were not so common at the time when they smacked me in the face.

I do not have my master's degree or doctorate in inspirational messaging. What I do have is a lifetime of hesitation in making the most of an opportunity. I often searched for an underlying motive. I am a cynic who has transformed into someone bursting to share his lessons with others who may not believe in the potential to change. I have been slowly turning from a "Doubting Thomas" to someone who believes in the ability of people to transform their negativity into something positive.

When I inadvertently became the teacher after all of these years, I was truly an advocate for self-change and was sharing my stories. I was not putting on an act. I began to truly feel like the person I wanted to be. I started to share my mistakes and people thanked me. Then it turned into sharing my accomplishments, and I saw how people wanted to take a similar path. I was being quoted in my own performance appraisals as being a role model.

I still had people giving me advice, and for the first time in my life, I was actively listening. I wanted to prove to everyone that I could do whatever I set my mind to—one person at a time. What I found was that I could have a larger impact on many people if I did it the right way. I was learning that my impact was reaching further than I thought. I could impact my small world or the large world. Whether you are working in a big company, a small office, or working from home, if you are working with others, you need to invest time in your own development in order to better yourself. This book is intentionally simple and is intended to serve as a reminder of all the great things I have learned in my professional life. I want you to use this book as one way to share my transformation with others—one reader at a time. Maybe you will share your lessons with others, too, when you are done reading it.

PART II
The Transformation

1.
Get a Mentor

Professional development comes from a lot of places. One place is from an individual you trust who can tell it to you straight. The trust and respect components in a mutually strong relationship can do wonders for your personal and professional growth. The process requires some strength on your part: you need to take the time with your mentor seriously enough to take the actions suggested by that mentor. Additionally, you must now invest more time in making a difference in your own career. Some people see this invested time as not important enough to make the commitment. Mentor relationships are not intended to just go through the motions. Although not all mentor relationships work out, I've rarely seen a situation in which something wasn't learned, even if it was a small lesson.

I've had multiple mentors throughout my career. The definition and intentions of a mentor are far and wide. How two people find each other is also an inconsistent variable. A mentor can be part of a formal work program that matches two people up based on skill, tenure, and ability. A mentor can be someone you look up to, admire, and respect. A mentor can also be someone you seek out for knowledge you currently do not possess, but want to gain. In all cases, a mentor relationship is special because you are being given a third party's perspective—one that is often completely different from your own thinking.

I started what I like to call a rotating mentor program for myself in 2008, which continues to be an active part of my ongoing development today. This self-directed program was a proactive approach to building my network and relationships. I often base my selection criteria on a need I have at the time, or on a particular business expectation. I have found the advantage of variety has been something I was seeking out in order to broaden my own business acumen.

Mentor relationships can be formal, meaning designated meeting

The Transformation of a Doubting Thomas

times and dates, or informal, meaning you connect through an already-established relationship based on a specific need. You might be surprised at the number of times you need a sounding board or simply objective advice from someone who does not have any vested interest in the game. The objectivity of a mentor gives you stability and sensibility to think straight, while keeping emotions in check.

Informal mentors are always good to have in your arsenal of tools. They are people you have worked with over time, in whose advice and suggestions you have a significant amount of confidence. Informal mentors are people to whom you can simply pick up the phone and say, "Please help me." The great thing about informal mentors is that typically the person is someone with whom you can release pent-up frustration or gather ideas immediately. I have built up relationships with many people throughout my organization. The people I go to most often know my capabilities and many times know just what to say, at just the right time. I have had many problems in the past related to my own stubbornness, thinking I could do everything on my own. The use of mentors is a continuous reminder that two heads are often better than one.

Mentors have become a key to my ongoing success. My number of connections continues to grow. The number of mentors is not as important as the variety of go-to people. As time goes on in my professional life, people have moved on from a direct working relationship to other areas of the company, while others have left the company. People no longer with your company are a great asset in a mentoring capacity. Whether you strike up a formal or informal relationship is not relevant. The objectivity of people you are seeking advice from means they most likely do not have the same emotional connection to the situation that you do, but still have enough familiarity with the business to provide meaningful guidance to assist you in whatever way you may need.

As someone who is involved in a mentor relationship, you need to put into it what you want to get out of it. I have known many mentor relationships that are simply two people catching up at a designated time and date. The instances when I have learned the most from mentors have been with the ones who have pressed me to stretch myself by giving me assignments and tasks for the next meeting. They often saw my ability and capacity well beyond my own expectations for myself. I was often being taught when I didn't even realize it.

These successful mentors also forced me to come up with the questions that drove the relationship. If you are in a mentor relationship, ask yourself the questions, "Why?" and, "What do you want to get out of it?" The answers will always vary based on the individual; however, there is always an answer. If you are unsure, use the questions to start the flow of the conversation with the mentor. The added value to the future meetings will begin to take hold. Someone has become your mentor for a reason. It is fair to ask tough questions of him or her and take advantage of the time together to gain from the knowledge, inspiration, and experience he or she can share. The challenge of solving difficult questions together will only build a deeper bond.

Finally, be patient as mentor relationships evolve. You may not always find the perfect match. The differences in opinions, styles, and knowledge that may be causing the strain in the relationship may also be the gap in learning you are seeking. You should take advantage of the situation, whether it is learning to deal with a different style or personality, or dealing with someone who has different expectations of the relationship. This should get you energized to learn to adapt, be patient, and make the most out of the relationship before you give up. Obviously, there is no prescription for the best time and definition of success between a mentor and student. Success may not be known until years from now, when you say, "I remember when my mentor (insert name here) told me that story about…"

I have also been in mentor relationships in which my mentor didn't do a lot. He or she multitasked during our time together and was not interested, or seemed preoccupied. You may say to yourself, "I would never be like that as a mentor if I was in a similar situation." You do not always have to have bells and whistles going off telling you this is the time to learn. If you remain active and engaged enough, and pay attention to what is going on around you, you will learn from these observations, so that when you are the mentor you will be fully invested. You may need to sever a mentor relationship that is not working, but you are still walking away stronger than you were before.

2.

Be a Mentor, and Learn Something Yourself

I never connected the dots about how much I missed leading people until I stopped managing them. I was finding teachable moments from lessons I had learned that needed to be expressed, and found I was lacking the people to tell. I think I found therapy in sharing all of my mistakes with others. I often told people regularly, "Don't step on any toes, don't burn any bridges, and keep the lines of communications open…because we will cross paths again." The purpose was to remind people that even if we part ways, we can still be there for each other.

Working for me was once described as swimming in the oceans of Maine. Initially, when you jump in, you are shocked and can barely move. After a while, you get used to it, are refreshed, and ultimately you learn to enjoy swimming in it. I had enough people tell me how much they learned under my management, but only after they had time to reflect on our time together (often many years later). Since at the time I held positions which involved more project management versus people management, I longed for the two-way dialogue of professional development conversations. Once I realized that I did, eventually, have a positive influence on people, I knew I wanted to at least be a mentor. As a mentor, I also came to the conclusion that the people I mentored—as opposed to those I managed—didn't have to listen to me, so I had to work harder to exert the right influence. I wanted to be a teacher again without having people wait years for that "aha" moment that they had learned something from me. I wanted to do it without throwing people into the ocean first.

It is interesting how people would come to me to say how they wanted me to teach their newer employees how to be better organized, or to teach managers how to be more direct. I underestimated the influence I was having on people who were eager to learn. By investing time with others with no strings attached, I began to naturally soften my directness

Be a Mentor, and Learn Something Yourself

because they had no vested interest in my teachings unless I could give them something impactful to walk away with. From an objective mentoring point of view, I could teach without forcing the issue. I could adapt my teachings based on what worked best for that person's style or situation.

I found myself more effective influencing others as I was learning myself. I found success in building bridges, and actively sharing my past successes and failures. Most importantly, I was becoming a better listener. I was growing more patient, and was no longer just hearing the words but was truly listening. I improved my communication skills by understanding the impact I had on others when I tried to speak over them or ignore their comments while I tried to come up with the next thing to say.

I was becoming someone else's sounding board. I could have put on my psychiatrist hat for some sessions. It depended on what the person I was mentoring at the time wanted or needed. I began to better adapt my advice and teachings based on the various situations. I became a stronger role model and a better mentor. Many people have invested their time and energy to share their knowledge with me as my mentors. I knew I wanted to do the same. Selfishly, I just couldn't—and still can't—get past the fact the every time I mentor someone, I walk away thanking them.

3.
Have Unprofessional Days — Gain Trust and Respect

Are you a person people trust and respect? That's a tough question to answer on your own because trust and respect can't be asked for—they must be earned. Trust and respect are also easy to lose. In my first year working, we had a person going through a management development program who covered our team in my manager's absence. The team was not listening to him. They were having side conversations in the middle of a staff meeting. The manager-wannabe screamed out, "You need to respect me." No, we did not *need to* respect him. In fact, whatever little respect we might have had was now gone. Respect can't simply be demanded.

The same is true for trust. Trust has to be gained. It takes a while for some people you are working with to truly trust you. However, in a company working toward a common objective and goal, it is critical to find the trust of the right people, especially people with whom you work closely. Of all my shortfalls, being ethical and trying to do the right thing were not one of them. Although I had issues earning respect from people who worked for me early in my career, trust seemed to be easier to gain. I needed to find a creative way to do both.

I am not a big fan of rumors, talking badly about people we work with, or yelling and screaming in the workplace. However, there are some days you want to bang your head against a wall. There have been occasions I have placed my phone on mute and stuck my tongue out at the computer. This is a very effective way to let off some steam and stem some frustration.

I found a creative way to earn both trust and respect. I used the trusting reputation I had, and gave people an ear during times they needed to vent. I have surprised many people working with me when they started down a tirade or sounded frustrated by openly encouraging the

Have Unprofessional Days—Gain Trust and Respect

conversation to go further. Depending on the day of the week this event would occur, I asked them if they wanted this to be "unprofessional Monday (or Tuesday, or Wednesday, or Thursday, or Friday)." As expected, I often caught people off guard with the question. However, the question often lightened the mood and allowed me to explain the opportunity that they could have a protected and supportive conversation to get them through the issue. What started as a joke to break up the frustration of a couple of individuals has now turned into a regular routine I have done for many years. I once had a person from Human Resources pull me to the side to "discuss" my "unprofessional Tuesdays." I thought I was about to get an earful from someone who frowned upon it. She started chuckling and commended me for creating an open environment, and made a comment that she might need to come see me herself for a couple of frustrating moments she wanted to get off her own chest.

The cleansing feeling of letting it all out eventually comes. First, it eases some tension the person may be feeling. However, most people start to tentatively tell me what's going on. Pent-up frustration soon turns into open dialogue. The discussion might start with problem dumping but most often turns into problem-solving sessions. When they know that what they've said behind closed doors (literally or figuratively) stays there in confidence, I earn their trust a little at a time.

In the long term, I am building credibility as a listener, a confidant, and nurturing the relationship with that person. The relationship aspect grows over time, which further allows more complex problem solving. By proactively offering my services to give the person a time and place, even unscheduled, to complain, I actually see the complaints diminish as the person learns to deal more effectively with his or her frustration levels.

This is not a wide-open invitation to "roll buses." However, I have found that this exercise allowed me to better understand the emotions people experience and how venting clears their heads. Once emotions are in check, the person becomes more objective in his or her thinking. People need to be comfortable in order to speak their minds. By providing an avenue for them to do that freely, they can become more effective in the short and long term, and you as a manager or mentor gain trust and respect.

4.

Dedicate Time Daily, Weekly, and Monthly to Writing Down Your Accomplishments— What Went Right?

One of my daughters could be with friends at school having the best time. Yet, when asked, "How was it?," or, "How was your day?" she will sometimes start with all of the things that went wrong or tell us the things she did not get the chance to do when they were together. Beyond the guilt staring me in the face at the idea that some of my negativity and cynicism had rubbed off on her, I realized there was a different approach to steer the conversation down a more positive path. I found success when asking her different questions, such as, "What was your favorite part of the day?" My previous generic questions had allowed her to start the conversation with a sour taste. The more targeted question with the positive overtones maneuvered the conversation to a better place from the beginning. Many times, the conversation ended positively because so much time and energy was dedicated to telling me what went right.

I invest time on my thirty-minute commute home daily to ask myself what went right and what was the day's biggest accomplishment? Success breeds success. I often document the successes when I get home. If an accomplishment is meaningful enough to write down, I will add it to my accomplishments folder or type it directly into my next performance appraisal self-assessment the next day.

I have time dedicated on my calendar monthly to organize my accomplishments. You can never be too busy to set aside time to pat yourself on the back every once in a while. I am not talking about hours of time. I am talking about a couple of minutes to write down a quick note, and then move on with your day. I've had many managers tell me how detailed my performance appraisals were. It comes across as a complete work that is often perceived to take hours of time, when in reality, it

Dedicate Time to Writing Down Your Accomplishments

is a simple routine that is pure brain dumping based on my wins.

I have also heard many peers complain when it was time to complete their own performance appraisals because they couldn't remember what they had accomplished, or didn't know where they would find the time needed to put it all together. They always saw that the deadline was fast approaching, and the procrastination had already caught up. I simply proofread and edit my performance appraisal self-assessment prior to the deadline and send it on. You might surprise yourself with the amount of work you have accomplished in that short period of time that you may have previously forgotten. You also get the benefit of reminding yourself of the many things you have done right.

If you do have people working for you or with you, and you are part of the sit-down, performance appraisal discussion, here is the next logical move: conduct the same routine for others that you do for yourself. Invest that same amount of time in keeping ongoing notes of your team's accomplishment for your input on their performance appraisals. Accomplishments for you and your people are often synonymous, due to the teamwork needed. The simple routine of maintaining detailed and noteworthy accomplishments and events gives you the chance to provide deserving people with the recognition they deserve. I have found that many of the details are forgotten by my team and are appreciated when they see that I didn't forget. Additionally, you lose the stress at performance appraisal time of a looming deadline ahead, since you are well prepared. Dedicating a small amount of time on a regular basis to tell yourself and people you work with that they are good at what they do allows you to enjoy the fruits of your labor. You simply proofread, edit, and send it on its way in a timely fashion to the people who need to know "what went right."

5.

Stop and Smell the Roses — or At Least Stop and Say Hi

We constantly hear how busy or stressed people are. Personally, I think this topic in the workplace has overtaken the weather as the top subject matter at the water cooler. In my opinion, we have all the time in the world—it is a matter of our choice of how to use it. We are running around manically picking up documents off the printer, emailing something important, multitasking, and jumping on conference calls. I get it. We have business to take care of.

I am a naturally fast walker. I like to get to places in a straight line and typically do not deviate from my path to get to my destination. I wouldn't say that I am always in a hurry, but I like to be efficient. The simple act of walking fast applied an unflattering label to me professionally. I was often accused of being unapproachable. Why? I was just going where I needed to be. I always seemed to give a quick smile, I thought.

What people see is all they have. They saw my eyes forward, the straight face saying, "I am on a mission." The quick smile was not enough to elicit a response. For the most part, there usually was something to do or a place to get to, but not always a "mission." I was unintentionally closing people out.

In all of our busy worlds, we have only a finite amount of time in each day. We must decide how to use that time. Some people like to get involved in social media (e.g., Twitter, Facebook, LinkedIn), while some like to text message the person at the desk next to them. The use of electronics and the ease of virtual communication have negatively impacted our ability to even want to have a personal conversation with the people we spend a lot of time with at work. Even with the case of electronic communications, we close people out when our faces are buried in our mobile devices checking emails or simply giving a head nod to someone while a cell phone is glued to our ears.

Stop and Smell the Roses—or At Least Stop and Say Hi

Ask yourself the question, "Do I know the name of my co-worker's spouse?" The message isn't to drop everything you are doing and become inefficient at work just to get to know someone's spouse's name, kids, or pets. The message is to take a couple of minutes, when it makes sense, to establish a relationship with the people you work with. In some cases, it may be to re-establish a relationship with someone at a different personal level. In addition to just making someone feel valued and appreciated, the personal aspect of the job has huge benefits to the professional side.

When I managed the hardest working people in any company, the front line people who worked directly with our customers, I learned to make it a point at the beginning of every day and at the end of every day to tap the chairs of the people I worked with to say hello and thank them for their efforts. I had seen a few very well respected, senior leaders do this for years. I started doing it myself because I wanted the perception of floor presence. I kept doing it because I learned so much about people just by asking about their weekends, the ball game, or the dance recital. It created new questions and discussions for other days. I liked to surprise people with a question about their sons or daughters, or ask about a sick relative. I didn't realize how much I was getting out of it, and how the people I worked with appreciated it.

The most important part was the thank you I wanted to provide them for coming in that day to take care of our customers. It seems like Management 101, but I must have missed that day of class early in my career. However, if it is fundamental management, then why was I one of the few people doing it in the management ranks? I actually put it on my calendar to walk on the floor at certain periods of time to thank them for their efforts.. The appointment pop-up in the midst of a typically busy day was a constant reminder that my success was directly tied to the people doing the hard work. People often thanked me for investing the short amount of time to do this. This observation also did not go unnoticed by them. Stop and smell the roses, and find the value of a simple greeting.

6.

Send a Note to Say Thank You, and Mean It

The typical email and instant message exchange at work ends with "thanks" or even "thx," to which the receiver responds, "np" (no problem). People are appreciative of the assistance and support they receive, but it often feels so ineffective because of the overuse of one word: "thanks." There seems to be no time or effort dedicated to it. Don't get me wrong—I'm sure the people I help are appreciative of my efforts. However, the perception of that quick "thanks" because it is more muscle memory than genuine recognition may take away from the heartfelt feeling of that appreciation.

If an instant "thanks" response came within seconds from the person you helped, it probably even caused a little extra effort on your part to go back in and delete it. I have caused some debate at work when I've broached the subject that I have a large amount of "real" emails I need to get to in a day. The point is that I like to be efficient and don't like to waste time. I don't want to be misinterpreted, because I like a pat on the back as much as anyone. However, I don't see the value of a message where someone took an extra six key strokes and hit send.

I have often struggled with addressing a lack of genuine sincerity of many of these quick and thankless "thanks" responses. My message is that if I do something for you in the course of my normal job responsibilities, I don't need the thank you—I will do it for you anyway. It may be my job, or I want to just help out a teammate. That is good enough for me. If I am constantly helping you out specifically, and you want to invest the time to individually thank me with a phone call or heartfelt email, I would appreciate the gesture and take notice of the invested time you took to do it.

The genuine meaning comes when the receiver perceives the feeling behind the sender's intentions to say thank you. When the sender adds a little note that mentions specifically what they thought was special from

Send a Note to Say Thank You, and Mean It

you, this little touch makes a world of difference. As a recipient, I feel more grateful for that type of note. As a sender of thank you notes, taking the small amount of time to handwrite one is also impactful. Likewise, adding a few sentences to an email or recognition note will add a smile to anyone's day.

In any case, I won't get into a contentious argument in the professional environment about the etiquette of all thank you delivery and methodology. I simply want to drive home the point to ensure that the recipient feels the effort that you put into thanking them.

Finally, the recognition should also be immediate. I have seen too many examples of formal recognition months after the event that triggered it. The instantaneous response shows you are paying attention—as long as it is more than "thx." I like to build time into my schedule once a week for about fifteen minutes to reflect upon the efforts of others to send notes based on recent performance. Try it—you will make someone's day. You do not have to thank every person for every email that you received in your inbox during the week. Try to think of a memorable experience and genuinely thank the people who deserve it—I bet you will have a smile on your face, too.

7.

Learn to Communicate Assertively

Many people internalize their thoughts and feelings. These thoughts may build up over time and cause pent-up frustration in the wrong circumstances. Some negative thoughts may gain momentum and may impact the future effectiveness of what you are trying to accomplish, and even impact a relationship that is being established because of a misunderstanding that needed clarification.

As stated previously, I have a tendency to be an introverted individual and have been known to internalize feelings. I have often said, to myself, "I wish they wouldn't do that," or, "I wish they would stop…," or, "I wish (fill in the blank)." I have had to make a concerted effort to push myself through these types of random thoughts, and make it a point to have a conversation, especially if I want to ensure that all parties involved are on the same page.

I was flying across the country on a last minute red-eye flight from California to New York. My originally scheduled flight had been cancelled due to foul weather. I'll even toss in the fact that I had been bumped up to first class before the other flight was cancelled. Since I had to switch airlines and make same-day arrangements, most of my normal preferences, such as window seat and front of the airplane, were not available. Unfortunately, I was given a middle seat on an airline that seemed to have smaller seats than I was used to. I was not in the most pleasant of moods as I boarded the plane.

A young woman approximately twenty-five years old was sitting next to me, to my right toward the aisle. On a flight that takes over five hours and flying through the night, I was ready to go to sleep. The airline was gracious enough to give us covers for our eyes and the seatbacks had televisions to watch when we were not sleeping. I began to warm up to the idea of this flight; until I closed my eyes for the first time. The young woman beside me was visibly nervous. She was jittery, shaking,

Learn to Communicate Assertively

twirling her hair, and constantly bumping into me, waking me up out of my light sleep. For two hours, I peered over her way to see her fixated on the Weather Channel. Each time the satellite picture showed the snow building up in New York, her body shook intensely. These weather updates came every twenty minutes. After being startled by her multiple times, and building up a frustration of, "Wait until I go home and tell my wife how miserable this flight was," I stopped myself. I took my eye cover off and my headset out, and asked her if she was all right. She said that she was nervous (no kidding). She feared she would miss her connection and be stranded in New York.

I started to calm myself down in an attempt to empathize with her situation. I began to have a conversation with her by asking more questions about her situation. I didn't want to spark a conversation for the sake of conversation. I had a purpose. I wanted to sleep and she looked like she needed a Plan B in New York. I had to be creative, but assertive enough to get there.

I used a level head to creatively determine what needed to occur to calm her down and create a game plan for her. I couldn't scream at her because I had a few hours left of the flight and I think the close proximity might cause a slight issue. I asked more direct questions, such as, "What is your biggest worry?" She mentioned she wasn't able to contact her parents in Virginia, who were going to pick her up after her connection. I asked her what I could do to help her, including assisting once we landed. We decided that we would go to the customer service desk to switch flights and I allowed her to use my cell phone to call her parents.

I started to think that I had a long time before I got home in order to complain to my wife about my terrible flight experience. I had a four hour layover until my next flight, so what did I have to lose by helping someone who obviously needed it? During my interaction with the young woman, I had to explain to her that worrying would not solve any of the issues, but actions would. I also realistically told her what I had coming up the next day, including a long drive after my final destination, and I needed the sleep. I was taking assertive steps that would have been difficult for me to take just a couple of years before.

She began to understand both sides. The young woman was gracious and appreciative of the advice and the assistance. I couldn't tell you how she did for the next few hours, because I slept like a baby. We landed and took care of the things she had been worrying about.

Communicating assertively does not mean you have to communicate aggressively. The message is to say what is on your mind at the time it is on your mind. It does not mean go ahead and scream and shout when

The Transformation of a Doubting Thomas

emotions are high. It does mean maintain a level head and state the facts, including what's in it for you and what's in it for them.

In another example, I took on a new position. I became the organizer of an important meeting and I wanted to impress my new co-workers by doing a good job. During the middle of the meeting, one of the leaders began to call me "Skippy." I thought it was odd the first time I heard it, but chose to ignore it. The second time I heard it, she was asking me to do something for her. I stopped, and gave a look that got an interesting reaction. I told her my name was Tom. I professionally asked her to call me by my name. She unprofessionally called me "Skippy" for a third time, and this time asked for the rest of the group to join in. Striving to get beyond the immature nature of the action, I simply responded again with a level head and said, "You can call me Tom, and if you want me to respond back, you can call me by my given name." This conversation was not pleasant, but it was needed if I wanted to establish myself appropriately with everyone there, including the one attempting to label me with a nickname.

Again, we both had something to gain. I needed early respect in my new role and she needed things from me to have the meeting run well. We both got what we wanted, including clear expectations and a real conversation.

I look back on the many times I allowed examples like this to fester and put me in a bad mood. All those times when I was swearing in my head and fuming at the person or situation, I could have been attempting to resolve the situation. I now realize there were times I allowed unnecessary things to go on in the workplace by simply internalizing my feelings of, "I wish it would stop…," but chose to do nothing about it. We should all be assertive when the need arises and watch problems get resolved. You may be surprised at the positive reception you get from the receiver of your message and you will appreciate your own ease in tension.

8.

Understand that Winning Isn't Everything— Losing Is

I have lost many things in the professional world. I have lost promotions. I have lost the next great position. I have lost confidence. I have lost my passion at times, and sometimes lost my way. The great news is that there have been very few times that I can remember when things did not work in my favor after a loss. If things did not work out as planned, I at least typically learned a valuable lesson. When I have lost, I have found myself building up my character, or something better has come along. The premise of this book is obviously my transformation based on key lessons during my professional career. This premise is based on many of my losses that really turned into wins—this book being one of them. You have two paths to take when you lose. You can get up and do something about it, or you can lick your wounds and do nothing.

I was asked to apply for a position that many thought I was qualified for in a call center. It was in a place where I had extended family close by, I was willing to relocate, and I had more than fifteen years of call center experience in quite a variety of roles. I was not an expert in the new field I would be entering, but I had taught myself all of the positions in the past and I was eager to learn a new one. The final candidates were narrowed down to three of us for two openings. Can you guess who was ranked number three?

The other two candidates had fifteen or more years in this particular business. I'm sure each of them was qualified for the job and would be great hires. I felt I could have had an advantage and could make a difference by sharing my diverse background, my experience from my other internal businesses, and my objectivity as an outsider to the business. The decision makers didn't think so.

I was upset after learning I did not get the job, but, knew I had to do something positive about the experience. Instead of accepting the,

The Transformation of a Doubting Thomas

"You didn't get the job" at face value, I dug in deeper with the decision maker. I learned through his feedback that I needed to sell my diverse background, my experience level, and creative objectivity better during the interviews. I was told I could have also networked more effectively in preparation for the interview process, and prepared differently. The difference with this lesson was that I stayed on the phone and had a real conversation about what I needed to do better the next time. I was asking questions and genuinely felt good after the conversation, reassured that I had been well thought of throughout the process, but I had room to improve for the next time. What I was beginning to realize was that the "next time" was all around me if I kept my eyes wide open.

Three days later, I heard about a brand new position that was in the works to increase employee retention. I proactively went after it. I produced a clear plan of attack to address the issue, spoke to the appropriate people about my interest, and utilized my background to effectively sell the point that I could build bridges across multiple businesses to expand the impact of the work. I didn't realize I would get to implement the feedback I had just received so quickly. I was given the job and taught a valuable lesson: certain things happen for a reason. I did have control of my career and could make a bigger impact to the overall company in my new role.

In another example, as an avid speech competitor with Toastmasters International, I have learned that competing helped to prepare me for the most stressful situations. The competitions also taught me how to clearly engage an audience for a short period of time, and showed me how to send a message that the audience would remember for a long time. I enjoy the challenge of these contests.

As I became more successful in the contests, I realized I needed to learn from my more-experienced fellow competitors. In addition to picking up many tips and learning how to broaden my style, I also learned to lose. Losing speech competitions was a great thing to push me to write a better speech, to prepare differently, and to get more people involved in the overall process by offering their input for the next competition. I knew I could always be better.

In the International Speech contest in the spring of 2010, I was the only competitor in my club who was available to continue in the next competition. I knew going in I would 'win' by default. I had practiced for over a month. You'll notice that I didn't say I *prepared well* for over a month. I practiced a speech that lacked a clear message for the audience. I finished in third place, out of three people. To increase the intensity of my loss, I found out that the second place finisher forgot he was in the

Understand that Winning Isn't Everything—Losing Is

competition until that day, and only practiced for forty-five minutes.

I was forced to rewrite my speech. Apparently, the weekend of the next contest must have been a bad date, because only two of us were there. Again, the top two progressed on to the next level. I had no idea if the changes I made worked or if I moved on by default again. I was not going to leave it up to the unknown. I asked everyone I knew what they thought. I presented the speech to my club more times than they probably wanted. I gave the speech as a guest to a club in Florida while I was traveling on business. I invested time each day on my week-long vacation with the family to fine tune my message. I interjected myself into a company meeting to spend seven minutes giving the speech because there was a large gathering of people. Everyone had an opinion, and I listened to them all. I placed second in the next contest and moved on to the regional finals. The final competitive speech of the season went well, even though I did not win the competition. However, I did win by gaining valuable experience and lessons. By losing, I had won. I lost to some fantastic speakers who gave me the encouragement to continue to drive myself. I was a better speaker, a better networker, and a more confident individual because of this experience. All of these lessons would prove to pay off in future competitions and within the workplace.

9.

Wait Three Months...

On what I remember was one of the most frustrating days I have ever had with a boss in my career, my wife had the gall to say, "Wait three months and one of you will be hired (into another role), fired, promoted, or demoted." It was her way of giving me a lesson in patience. I had come home after another bad day with my boss. For many reasons, including differences in management styles, personalities, and personal goals, I just didn't get along with this particular boss. The thought had seriously crossed my mind to leave the company.

As I had found through my research with employee retention, most people choose to leave their manager rather than leaving the company. My wife was right. I needed to hang in there and things would change. Things did happen quickly. My hated boss was 'double' promoted into a different position. I didn't even think it was possible, but it happened. I could not have been happier for myself and for the fact that the person moved on. The new person who came in gave me a clean slate. He listened to my ideas and gave me opportunities to drive the business and grow.

We all know that promotions in companies do not always come quickly or easily. The message is not to sit around and wait for something to happen. Opportunities are few and far between before someone is tapped on the shoulder. The message of "wait three months" is also a call to action to build the relationship, even if it is damaged. Some of my most constructive conversations have come when I have directly said to someone, "I think we got off to a rough beginning. Do you mind if we start over," or "I think there is some misunderstanding between us." By making the first move in reaching out to smooth over a rough relationship, I have found that many people are receptive to at least listening. Many times, we had a good laugh together over the original situation as time went on.

The "three month" concept is a good reminder that time is always ticking forward and can work in your favor. Businesses are always

Wait Three Months…

changing and this concept shows that you can be part of the change. By exhibiting patience with a level head, and taking action to strengthen bonds and relationships, you will move forward to success in your overall career beyond those three months.

10.

Stand Up for What's Right

Similar to communicating assertively, you have the right to show your character and integrity. There are times where you can't—and should not—accept what is going on around you. You may not always get your way, but you will know in your heart and your head that you did the right thing. If you are anything like me, you have the pull of guilt during situations in which you've said to yourself, "I should have done that differently."

One of those guilty moments that I have carried with me for years is a performance appraisal conversation I had with one of my employees. She always had been bright and creative, and exhibited great people skills in my eyes. She was likeable, but was often seen as too soft and lacking the ability to drive performance. Many of her past managers carried this perception and managed her by providing feedback to be more direct and have more forceful conversations with her subordinates.

After some of my own observations, and a significant amount of time together using open-ended questions to bring out her strengths and opportunities, we both came to a mutual agreement that there wasn't a need to drive people harder. What she needed to do was understand the reporting and analytics of the business better in order to better target performance discussions with her people. This "aha" breakthrough moment was important to building our relationship as manager and employer. We both felt good over the outcome of our intense conversations and started to see improvement.

At performance review time, my scores for her were lowered by upper management. One senior leader had clung to the older perception that she needed to have more forceful conversations to drive performance. I "tried" to persuade the senior manager to increase the scores back to where they had been. Looking back on my argument, it was more emotion based and lacked enough substance to make a difference.

Stand Up for What's Right

The conversation to pass on the lowered score to my employee was extremely difficult, to say the least. The reason for the difficulty was my problem. First, I had not properly prepared her for the discussion, because we both felt like we were on the same page with our assessment of her performance. Second, I was telling someone else's story. I tried to communicate the corporate direction, but did not believe it myself; and she knew it. I did not want to come right out and say to her, I scored you higher and I disagree with my manager. The conversation was a mess. As I have pondered this conversation in my head many times over the years, I've realized that I had facts and figures to show her team's improvement. Not only did I have her team's results, I had action plans that she and I were working on that clearly identified her specific opportunity. My argument to increase her scores was glossed over with too much generalization and did not give me the facts to clearly make my points.

She was obviously upset. I found out later that she seriously considered leaving the company. Who could blame her? Do you want to work for a company that does not judge you on your true merits? During the conversation, she maintained more maturity and composure than I would have expected of anyone in that circumstance.

Although she constantly reminds me years later of that conversation, it is more jovial because she has seen my genuine learning and belief that she was better than she was scored. I learned to manage others differently based on that conversation, and I saw in her a confidence that she could prove people, like the senior leader, wrong. It showed me her strength—a strength I needed personally. Our personal relationship grew over the years and we became close. We have bounced ideas off of each other and became informal mentors as our professional paths grew apart.

She took the high road. I now make sure that I do as well. I have a card she sent to me a couple of years later. It appeared out of the blue. It was a simple hello card. She wrote in it that she wanted to thank me for taking the time to teach her about leadership, integrity, and attitude. She mentioned in the note that she appreciated the encouragement and challenge to grow. She even added, "For kicking me when I needed it." I wish I had beaten her to the punch. I should have thanked her for her leadership in a time when she was a subordinate, for her integrity when she knew I was having conflicting thoughts, and for her positive attitude during a trying time. She "kick" started me into understanding how to act in a tough corporate environment. When there are times I feel the pull to go back to old habits, I just turn around and re-read the card. I have done this dozens of times to put myself back on track.

In an interesting twist, the senior manager who did not believe in

The Transformation of a Doubting Thomas

her at the time brought her back to his line of business several years later. He clearly saw her leadership abilities by then. He showed his ability to be open to admitting he was wrong so many years before, and he needed someone who showed heart and character. She had always been willing to learn and adapt. He finally saw that and was able to utilize her maturity to assist in leading other less experienced managers.

11.

Differentiate Yourself—Make It Known

Too many times in the professional work place, we try too hard to conform and fit in. We do not want to rock the boat or make waves. It is human nature to want to fit in and be a part of something. If you don't believe me, think back to your freshman year in high school. As a new employee, we are typically learning something new and do not want to make any mistakes…Or at least any big ones. We may want to simply blend in. As time goes on, blending in becomes part of the fabric and habits we've built.

When I first started my career in banking, I had success with my performance on the phones. I was able to take advantage of not being face to face in an interaction. I could quietly and effectively have phone conversations with my customers. My performance was consistent and I began to be recognized on a regular basis in front of my peers. I was asked to increase my job responsibilities and expand my role. I would be taught to assist with the reporting, and asked to spend time with peers who were struggling.

During my performance appraisals or the occasional internal job interview, I still sold myself short in describing what I did. If I was collecting bad loans, I would simply say I tried to help customers with their financial difficulties. I didn't realize that I could be special and different among a sea of people with the same job responsibilities. With hundreds of collectors, everyone could give a generic job responsibility answer of, "I try to help customers with their financial difficulties." This was a starting point but interviewers, future managers, and company decision makers wanted to hear more from someone willing to differentiate himself. What's interesting is that I could not identify this need myself and did not pick up on any cues given to me to stand out. I would get direction to work hard, hit my goals, and sometimes hear the phrase "try to stand out." I always interpreted this as making more 'widgets,' going faster, and working longer, but not necessarily describing how I could differentiate myself. As much as we don't want to think about it, we are always on

The Transformation of a Doubting Thomas

stage, and—in many cases—in competition. This isn't an invitation to step on others' backs as you climb the corporate ladder. However, you do have an invitation to give yourself some credit when it is deserved, and be prepared to be your own elevator when the time is right.

I applied for an internal management development program in my second year at MBNA. The program accepted fifteen leaders. I went through at least seven interviews with senior members of the company. Can you guess what number I was? I was number sixteen. Candidates aren't typically told where they finished after the interview process, but the people who nominated me wanted to help explain why I didn't get it. I was told I had the skills and that I was on the edge of being selected.

I said that this was unfortunate because I thought my performance spoke for itself. In collections, I was the top performer nine times out of the twelve months. I was doing extra work on the side to assist the manager, and had recently completed a manager-selected program in which our group made some significant recommendations that would improve our business. I told the person giving me the feedback that it was all there on my résumé. The decision-maker said many résumés, especially after only two years of internal experience, looked alike and I should have brought these facts to light. There are few times in your life that you should assume anything. This type of situation was one of them. I was given feedback to not assume that they had any knowledge of me, had read my résumé, background, or application, and that I needed to bring that information to the forefront.

I began sharing with everyone the saying, "It is not bragging if it is a fact." Stating your own facts, when timed and communicated appropriately, is acceptable. I am not overly confident to begin with; therefore, I do not typically come across as cocky. However, the inverse is that I have come across as plain and non-descriptive. You should be proactive in order to find your way of differentiating yourself and make sure the people you work with know it.

We are all special in our own way. Yes, this is a cliché, but still holds true. The message here is to bring out what makes us special and different in our interactions with others. In my mentoring sessions, I will often ask the people I am working with what they accomplished during the month. I often get typical answers such as, "Not a whole lot," or, "Nothing different or out of the ordinary." When I keep digging deeper, I find that they were involved in a project that saved thousands (or millions) of dollars, helped out an extremely frustrated customer, or asked to assist on a project team. Did everyone else accomplish these exact things, too? The answer is often no. You don't have to brag and shout from your rooftops

Differentiate Yourself—Make It Known

telling the whole world what you have done. However, you need to realize the difference between your day-to-day functions and what makes you who you are. As a mentor and manager, I have made it my mission to exert the effort to have people spill their guts to me when it comes to their accomplishments. I encourage people to proactively share their highlights and get used to telling their own special story.

I would often ask my direct reports to submit their accomplishments on a monthly basis. There were many months when I could put two side by side, and they would look very similar. The side-by-side exercise is what started to get me thinking about how to teach the people who worked for me how to reach for higher goals and therefore put more meaningful accomplishments down on paper.

We started to share more accomplishments openly in our staff meetings. The purpose was not for competitive reasons, but to share best practices. I would often praise them, and emphasize that being creative and innovative in order to make the team better made everyone stronger. I believe that the courage to try new things, whether or not it worked, is in itself an accomplishment.

When we had managerial requirements to go back on the phones for four hours a month, my employees often listed the requirement as one of their accomplishments. I would ask them what they truly accomplished by doing that? If they answered, "Met the requirement," they were not getting the full picture and I had more work to do to teach them. If they gave an example of how they resolved a sticky situation with a customer or mentioned how they now understood what the front-line associates were complaining about relating to their computer system and had a solution to fix it, they were differentiating themselves as leaders.

No two people are the same. I am very proud to list out the various jobs I have worked. I can say that no one has followed my career trajectory. I would often joke around, saying that I couldn't keep a job. I wasn't sure if people were kicking me out or if people really wanted me. As I thought about this more seriously, I realized that early in my career, people were indeed 'kicking me out.' They were attempting to have me get more experience and to play to my strengths—the things that made me special…made me different. I realized later in my career that this was still true to some extent, with more weight on people really wanting me. People wanted me because of my diverse background and the broad knowledge I could bring to their business. I could bring best practices, creativity, and freshness to jumpstart some spinning wheels. What makes you special? Does everyone know it?

12.

Be Impatiently Patient

Maybe I will do it tomorrow. 'It' could be anything. Tomorrow I will set my goals. Tomorrow I will earn the big promotion. Tomorrow I will write the next great novel. Some of us keep wishing and some of us allow frustration to build up. Still, we take no action, except maybe a complaint or two, or maybe three. We have all heard that good things come to those who wait. However, I will tack on that great things will come to those who earn it and take action.

I have had many career conversations with individuals who complained that his or her manager had rarely, if ever, had a career development conversation with him or her. The complaints include comments that his or her manager has performance-based conversations that help with the present, but lack the long-term discussion to push them further in their careers. I have seen consistent focus group feedback and anonymous survey feedback reiterating the same thing.

I have had to provide some tough feedback to people by asking them, "When was the last time you read your performance appraisal?" A very large percentage of people I ask have answered that it was the day it was administered. People have a silver tray of feedback on their lap that they think they can memorize after a thirty to sixty-minute discussion. They are wrong. People need to reinforce the constructive feedback that will make them better. They should not wait for the next performance review that will take place six months to a year from the last one. People should take hold of that feedback and take action immediately. Grab the feedback head on and start to implement the actions needed to make you stronger. Be impatiently patient to make yourself better.

If the complaints are accurate and you are really not getting career advice or long-term direction, you have the right to understand and ask for it. You need to know exactly what it takes to get promoted or get to the next level, or even what it takes to maintain great performance results.

The conversation does not have to be contentious or even demanding. A simple request of, "Can you help me to better understand what it takes…" can go a long way.

Everyone should do their homework to at least know the minimum requirements and expectations for their current role and what is needed to get to the next level. My former company used to have minimum requirements to get promoted to certain officer positions, including taking certain courses, and submitting at least one original, formal, creative idea annually to make the business better. I would be amazed any time I had a conversation with a colleague who said he or she could not come up with a fresh idea or find the time to take the training courses.

The irony may be that the driving force for me early in my career was my inability to take accountability. I was driven to cover my bases for all minimum requirements to ensure that never happened to me. I refused to allow any decision maker to make an easy decision to count me out of the running for an officer promotion simply because I had not met the check-box requirements. That would make it too easy for others. Remember, I was in the habit of blaming others.

I was learning that if I was going to blame someone for not promoting me or giving me the next great role, I wanted to force the conversation to be more meaningful than, "Sorry, you missed the minimum requirements." The drive to meet the requirements forced me to be impatiently patient because I was going to meet all of my annual requirements in January (if the cycle started at the beginning of the year), as soon as I saw it in my inbox, or as soon as physically possible to complete.

My concerns for missing small details or requirements, or gaining a reputation as a procrastinator, were not part of my personality. My fear of missing a deadline or not completing my workload actually enhanced the perception of me in the eyes of many leaders. I was gaining a reputation for getting things done quickly. I was also becoming known for reading the details that may have been glossed over by others. I was building a positive reputation based on my emerging skill set.

Although others were still getting promoted around me, it was not because I wasn't meeting my goals. It was the many other components that had been reiterated many times over. My inability or slow adaptation to change how I got the job done was holding me back (e.g., relationship building, cynicism). The positive momentum change in how I was viewed in getting things done quickly was a good sign toward future advancements.

I would eventually find my way to meeting many of my professional goals, but it was not within my personal, unwritten time frames. I was

The Transformation of a Doubting Thomas

beginning to be more driven and more specific in establishing these goals. I would set a certain age at which I wanted to achieve a title or position. There were designated times when I wanted to expand my role. I was often close, but I was not always within my personal deadlines. I was all right with that because my impatience was driving me to take the better road to eventually get to the position or goal I wanted.

In fact, there were at least two times in my career where I was in the right place at the wrong time. I was given expanded responsibilities at a time when I was not fully prepared for the positions. In both cases, I was asked to step back to a lesser role or change my position completely. I also learned that getting exactly what you want at the wrong time can have devastating impacts professionally. I learned from both scenarios to set clear goals, but be prepared for when I get there.

The lessons of not only knowing what I wanted, but also when I wanted to get there, proved valuable. My impatience made me do more homework and research to set aggressive, but more realistic, goals. I knew myself better than anyone else and I began writing out a game plan to help me achieve my goals. Doing things on the fly and just pushing to get someplace fast happened far too many times early in my career, to my detriment. I had the drive to get there quickly, but I lacked the specificity of where I was heading. This held me back. I needed to know where I wanted to go and be impatiently patient to get there—with a plan.

Finally, if you are fortunate enough to take on a new role, you need to be impatiently patient in learning the business. You can never passively wait to meet the learning curve within a given time frame in a new position. First, you need to understand the business is moving quickly and can't wait around for you. Second, if you are effective in attacking the transition, you can accelerate your ascent to gain technical knowledge. Your patient efforts to impatiently learn the business as quickly as possible will assist you in gaining credibility with the people you are working with as you gain insights on the integration between different faces of the business, technology, culture, and styles. Take advantage of a learning curve if there is one, but learn as quickly as possible by using the people and resources around you to absorb everything.

13.

Prove People Wrong

I was about to start this section as "prove negative people wrong," but realized that not all situations involve a negative person. Some just involve an honest person strong enough to tell you something you may not want to hear, but need to hear. Years ago, I was growing tired of my computer programming position. I had been in the role for only three months. The computer programming assignment was more a move to get me out of my previous job than a move because the job was a great fit for me. It was not a match made in heaven for a communication major with no computer expertise.

I knew I needed a change. I became more dissatisfied with my job as I realized that it was not the proper career path for me and I had a steep learning curve in a position I was not motivated to pursue. The experience was good in teaching me that this role was not for me. I am glad for the time because I was put in the shoes of people who do this difficult job of getting calls only when something is broken or receiving the urgent request when someone needed it yesterday.

I surprised myself by proactively setting up a meeting with the senior executive to see what it would take to transfer somewhere else—anywhere else, actually—to become a manager of people again. My approach was not to complain about what I was doing at this point in my career, because as much as I disliked it, I was still doing a valuable function.

If you recall, this was the time in my career when I was removed as a manager because I, the "interpersonal communications major" could not relate well with people. The senior leader said he did not see me successfully leading people. He would not let me manage again because he could not see me as someone who could lead an entire department. He wanted someone in whom he could see true leadership material. He needed to see the potential of a candidate two positions ahead, not just in the next promotion. He said he did not see that potential in me as a leader, and

The Transformation of a Doubting Thomas

denied my request. I can't blame him. My reputation was not stellar when it came to people management at the time.

As I look at it now, he was being direct and honest; something I crave now. I spent many years bitterly and conveniently remembering a different tone and context: he was out to get me, and I needed to prove him wrong. Although I genuinely believed he did not like me or want to see me succeed, I realize now that I created my own perception of the conversation to fit my need to be motivated. I needed the rejection to push me further to succeed.

There are two things you can do when you get tough feedback you don't want, but need to hear. You can do nothing. Nothing can also be expanded to complain about it, be frustrated by it, and do not seek a solution. The other option is to accept it and make the most of it. You can use the feedback to make yourself better and stronger. You can build character and put yourself into a better position to succeed. Direct and honest feedback does not come as often as we like. There is value in it and we should absorb as much of it as possible.

I believe that that interaction with the senior executive that lasted no more than ten minutes saved my career. I had a specific focus point to motivate me. I must have thought about it every day for over five years. It drove me. It pushed me harder. It became my driving force to rally at a time when I was ready to walk out the door. My wife reminds me now that my misery and frustration were growing so much that if I hadn't changed my career course at that time, we probably wouldn't have stayed together long enough to marry. In simple terms, I was getting on her nerves with my constant complaining.

The manager who chose not to give me another chance in a manager role did offer me a chance to support a newly-formed business in another state. I would not be managing people. However, I now had the drive to prove him wrong. I did have the added motivation on the personal front of being newly engaged to a great woman, and I wanted to have a great life with my soon-to-be wife.

Being told I could not do something or was not good enough drove me to seek out the answers I needed to improve and eventually get where I wanted to be. As often as I thought about it bitterly for so many years, I am thankful for the courage the person had to tell me what I had to hear, and I am appreciative for the extra kick I needed to want to prove to everyone that I could do whatever I set my mind to. I needed to prove the people wrong who said I wasn't ready for it. More importantly, I needed to make the doubt in my own abilities go away. I needed to prove *myself* wrong. I stopped thinking about that fateful conversation every day when

Prove People Wrong

I got my first job managing managers about five years later. I reached my goal with hard work and a push toward transforming myself into the person I wanted to be and toward the person I knew I was capable of being. I proved him wrong. I wonder now if he was trying to motivate me from the start.

14.

Prove People Right

When you are working with many people in an office, find positive people who support you, then stick with them. There will always be some level of negativity, all with varying degrees, in an office—nobody is perfect and mistakes are made. The question is, what is done to keep it alive and what is done to make it go away? Sometimes, the negativity is short lived because a sale was lost or a promotion was missed and people quickly got over it. In some cases, it is more long term, because of an economic recession, for example, during which people need more nurturing and support to find their way through. Negativity can start with an individual and quickly gain momentum to a group. Negativity has a tendency to grow like a cancer and build upon itself if the people affected don't make a conscious effort to stem the tide. We all have the choice to take action and surround ourselves with the types of people who want us to succeed, provide us constant support, and build a positive working environment.

In my early career, it seemed fun to sit around at lunch time and find things to complain about. One day, we would complain about the boss, the next day it may be a colleague, and the following day it may be a customer. I thought it was good therapy to get it all out and move on. However, we did not move on from the complaining. Even conversations about the weather were complaints about how hot and humid it was in the summer and how cold and miserable it was in the winter. My crowd of complainers built off the negative momentum. I found most of our conversations continued to have the same thread of negativity being pulled through.

What was interesting is how much my long-term mood and outlook changed based on who I was working with and spending most of my time with. As I took on more independent roles, I had more choices to decide who I would spend time with. I took less group lunches and started to separate myself from the companions who I felt were adding to the negative environment.

I was also learning to establish new relationships and networks. With my newer relationships, I was less comfortable openly complaining, and found myself not getting caught up in a flow of negative dialogue. I found that as I was meeting more new people, I wanted to spread positive messages. One of those ways was to proactively recognize the work of the people I was spending more time with. When co-workers are across the country, it is nice to have a recognition email waiting for them. I started to also realize that it was becoming easier to compliment the people I was working with locally because spreading a positive message was becoming contagious for me.

I started to surround myself with similar people who sought to see the glass as half full. I still had my moments of doubt and negativity, but the moments were less frequent. That doesn't mean that I stopped providing critical and balanced feedback when appropriate. It just means it was easier to provide constructive feedback when people trusted the source as someone who was looking out for their best interest. In fact, I believe my feedback was more useful since there was more sincerity behind it as opposed to entering a complaint session.

I knew I was making a difference and was being perceived differently when people came out and said, "Your stock is rising." I had such a feeling of satisfaction that someone would outwardly say that to me. I actually heard this more than once from several people I knew believed in me and supported me. I had a trusted group of people who looked out for my best interest and kept me focused on seeing the best in everything.

I found a network of people who saw my strengths and maximized the use of those strengths. I wanted to spend more time with them because I fed off the positive energy. They believed in me and saw a path to success. I thought I was getting more roles that played off my strengths. In reality, this was true, but not to the extent I originally believed. I was not just in positions playing to my strengths—I was working smarter to expand on these strengths, and turning my weaknesses to strengths. For example, in the past, I may not have had the confidence to question something that did not make sense. When I was surrounded by people who encouraged me to ask open-ended clarification questions, I came up the learning curve more quickly, and gained confidence.

In another example, I was sent to a new manager and felt like I had to start over again. As previously mentioned, there were times when I was moved to different roles in my career when I wasn't succeeding. In this case, my new manager said in our first conversation that I was taking

The Transformation of a Doubting Thomas

over the forty-fifth ranked team in the company. His instructions were simple: "Make them number one." He mentioned that he trusted me and would give me space as long as he saw the team's growth. He was giving me a clean slate. As we continued to work together, he was making me believe in myself again. I was starting to take the right actions to have the team believe in me, too. The team rose to the second-ranked team in the company in less than two months. I was riding their coat tails, while being there to provide support and encouragement. I was proving my new manager right.

You can start to prove people right by finding the motivational factors to not let that someone down or by making the extra effort to show them what you are capable of. In all cases, your own success is facilitated when you surround yourself with good people who support you, people who believe in you, people who encourage you, and people who inspire you. Fend off the negative people who may be nearby, find the uplifting people, and together create your own positive vision by feeding off the positive energy and enthusiasm of others. Then, prove them right.

15.

Have Multiple and Diverse Role Models

We work with many people who set the right example. They may not be perfect but there is something about them we want to emulate. Take a careful look at them and see what styles and skills may work for you. Seek out the great things they have that you can grab hold of and add to your own abilities.

When it comes to role models, we sometimes think in singular terms. We pick out the one person we want to be most like and sometimes try to emulate them. This narrows down our own potential and might pigeonhole what we are trying to accomplish. Seek out multiple role models who have a wide variety of skills. A diverse set of role models will open more possibilities for adoption into your own routine and expand your proficiency. As stated in an earlier passage, you want to maintain your own uniqueness and it is important to maintain your differentiating factors. We don't want you looking to be a clone or a wannabe, but we would be leaving an opportunity on the table if we didn't become keen observers to role models around us. We can always find best practices to share and pick up good habits and styles that work for us.

A role model differs from a mentor because there is typically less interaction—or the opposite, constant interaction because you work closely with them. Whether you are monitoring them from up close or afar, you should take note of what makes them successful.

My first real taste in a role model was a peer of mine named John. John was the person who swapped jobs with me when I was told I needed to do something different after my first managerial stint. John was the computer programmer who was looking for a change. I was the manager not cutting it in the eyes of the leadership. Apparently, the timing was perfect. I disliked John for a variety of reasons. First, he was right next door and I saw every move he made. Second, he was a nice guy and people seemed to be having fun and working harder for him than they

The Transformation of a Doubting Thomas

had for me. I realized my distaste was actually jealousy. I began to watch him from next door with a new lens and began to learn what I had done wrong when I had overseen the team.

Many of the things he was doing to earn the respect of the people came down to managing the details. He was spending individual time with the people and maximizing his floor presence. He was practicing what I now see as fundamental in people management, but was too close—or too inexperienced—to practice when I first started managing. I was learning to study John in action, and it was fascinating. I began to understand that he was an unintentional role model who was teaching me. Watching his success early on was hard for me. As the years went on, I started to do what I had seen him do and began to see my own similar success. I began to make sure that I included this story in all of my mentoring sessions and leadership teaching sessions.

I have since targeted other role models based on my specific needs. The person who first called me a cynic has taught me about accountability, ownership, and leadership. At a social gathering, my wife asked him what he liked about his job. His response was simple and concise. He said, "I like being accountable. I like making decisions." He is a true leader who understands that people depend on his direction and his ability to make decisions, and then act on them. He is also a fantastic leader and communicator who can rally a group of people to go on any difficult mission together. In the worst of times, people turn to him for a clear and motivational message that leaves no question as to which way they should go.

I have a good friend who I met early in my career. He taught me how to be selfless and giving. Additionally, he was the person who looked past all of the negative perceptions others had of me. He took a chance on me when I was young and inexperienced. He took an active approach to listening to my ideas and wanted to know my opinions to make the business better. He trusted me and respected me, even when I still felt people were out to get me. He gave me a sense of confidence that I truly could be a leader.

There are countless other role models who have taught me the value of technical job knowledge and being an industry leader in certain banking fields. There are other leaders who have taught me the value of being straightforward and speaking from the heart. There are still others who inspire me and give me confidence just by watching them.

There is also a small pocket of people you observe, and say to yourself, "I don't want to be like them." This group of people may be just as valuable for your own growth. When I was struggling in a trial position

Have Multiple and Diverse Role Models

leading a group of managers, I could not seem to communicate well with my boss. I believe this was due to the fear factor he instilled in me. He attempted to drive my performance by yelling and screaming at me in the hopes that this fear would make me do things better. If he had just understood my wants, needs, and expectations, he would have figured out that I would work hard and do the job anyway. He could have put his efforts and wasted energy elsewhere to make the team better.

Instead, there was constant pressure put on me. His favorite routine, or game, seemed to happen every Friday afternoon around five o'clock P.M. He would call me to come see him in his office. Apparently, after a very long week, he wanted to ensure that I had a miserable weekend of fuming over his last instructions or put downs regarding what I hadn't accomplished during the week. I vowed I would never be like him. He became my role model antithesis.

Another role model I worked for was bright and he knew how to dig deep into a business to reduce expenses and increase profits. He also lacked people skills and held on to original opinions for a long time. Once he formulated an opinion of you it was permanent. As I learned the basics of running larger operations from him, I still struggled early in my career in grasping the people-management skills. He was not afraid to make me aware of this shortcoming. The irony was that he could observe poor people skills, but didn't ever see them in himself. When I finally got out from under his management and saw some success managing others, he refused to see any of my growth or acknowledge any of my recent accomplishments. I had an interview with him about five years later for a job overseeing a fairly large unit. He only continued to bring up my failures from those days when I had been inexperienced and directly working for him. He said (paraphrased), "It sounds like you have done some good things, but I can't get past the time when you…" He must have mentioned my past on at least three occasions. In the middle of the interview he said he was hungry and wanted to go to the café to grab a sandwich. I had to have a walking interview while he took care of himself. He lacked the ability to have an open mind or change judgments of me, and still had no self-awareness or was just pompous. After he refused to give me the job in his area, I vowed to never be like that. He was the perfect negative role model. I knew I had to begin to withhold my personal judgments of others, see other people's growth, and be willing to give people second chances.

We have an advantage of seeing what goes on around us each day. Use these observations as a tool for your own development. Watch the people around you with a critical eye, and become aware of the diverse and sheer

The Transformation of a Doubting Thomas

number of role models surrounding you. They will teach you a lot about who you are and who you can be. In some cases, you will acknowledge characteristics from people you want to emulate, and in other cases, find the characteristics you want to avoid. Be on the lookout for your next teaching moment—your role model may be right there in front of you.

16.

Write Down Your Goals…in Pencil

I have heard on more than one occasion that an extremely small number of people have specific written goals—as low as five percent. As another way to differentiate yourself, be among the five percent to lay out your path for success on paper. Whether it is personal, professional, academic, health, or any other aspects of your life, you should write out your goals.

The likelihood of you taking the appropriate actions to achieve the goals goes up exponentially when you have them written. The goals should be specific so you know if and when they have been accomplished. Each goal needs to also be aggressive or it is not worth shooting for. The aggressive goal, however, should not be so far out of reach that it is not attainable. You should set progressive goals so you can see the small wins piling up. You need to understand that you may not achieve one-hundred percent of them—at least on the first try. The idea that you can go back to achieve a missed goal may refine the quality and outcome of what you are trying to accomplish. The fact that they are written allows you to see your progress and creates action plans to attain them.

If you achieve your goals, you should build on those successes and set more goals. These goals should be expandable for future steps. For example, I wanted to progress up through all of the phone positions in my line of business, and then move on to the somewhat natural progression of assistant manager, manager, and beyond. The goal of what I wanted to accomplish was set.

In addition, I set timelines for when I wanted to achieve them. The timeline has always been the hardest part for me. I have always wanted to get to each of the next steps as quickly as possible. There were many hurdles that delayed my ability to achieve my goals and I missed many of my expected timelines.

When establishing timelines, you need to account for potential

The Transformation of a Doubting Thomas

roadblocks. Not everything will be clearly laid out for you. As previously stated, there were the two times in my career when I was asked to move in the other direction, to lower roles, because leadership didn't feel I was effective or prepared for the additional responsibilities. There were also the times I felt ready to move up but did not interview well. Regardless of the reasons, I needed to reset my goals.

Resetting the goals means many things. It might mean resetting the timeline to the same goal and staying on course. Resetting the goal may mean adjusting the goal metric itself to move in a different direction. This is not always the easiest thing to do, since you may be unfamiliar with the road you are looking down. As stated earlier, pull back on the aggressive time frames, scale, or intensity of your goals, and set the goals in smaller increments. Again, the increments should be realistic and challenging. The key message is to write down your goals and know they will evolve. Goal setting should be dynamic and fluid. More than twenty years after leaving college as a communication major, I had no idea I would have gone through so many aspects of the financial industry. When you write out your goals, I would suggest using a pencil.

17.

Control What You Can Control (You Have More Control Than You Think)

You should stop and ask yourself what you truly have control over. You may find yourself starting down a path of those things you can't control, such as the weather and the stock market (at least not by yourself). You also can't control whether or not other people talk about you, so you might as well give them something good to talk about. If you are part of a large organization, you can't always control something happening in other parts of the company where you don't have oversight. All of these uncontrollable factors may impact your satisfaction level, your frustration level, and your ability to make a difference. You need to trust that your teammates will get the pieces of their job done and be a good partner who will be there to assist when the need does arise.

You should focus on your own little world and the sphere of control you do have. Start with just thinking of you. You have control over your attitude, whether you take action, whether you speak up, and whether you want to offer your ideas. You may not be able to control the root cause of your stress and frustration, but you can control how you deal with that root cause.

There are plenty of factors to consider regarding what you do have control over. What is your patience level? What is your acceptance level that you can and will have an impact on the bigger picture? Are you open and willing to put yourself out there when you are not in your comfort zone? What is your acceptance to learning from your mistakes? How willing are you to put in the effort to transform yourself into someone in a better position to impact the things you can control?

I worked for a company in which people were very loyal and were leaders in the industry. As a whole, we were confident and convinced that nobody could run this type of business as well as we could. When the company was bought, it was devastating. Although the buyout saved

The Transformation of a Doubting Thomas

us from ruin, we still had people walking around saying, "Who bought who?" There was a population of employees convinced that they were better than everyone, though this was just one reaction among many. Some people froze in fear of losing their jobs, while others took a more proactive approach by dusting off their résumés. I personally called a relative who worked for our new company. Her company had been acquired a few years earlier. Her advice was to control what I could control. She even mentioned that with a company this large, I might actually find more opportunities to thrive with a decent attitude. It seemed counterintuitive at the time, but she was right.

How could my small voice control anything in a company so large and that seemed constantly in flux? I began by trying to understand the new company mission and culture. Although this seems basic, the old company had an extremely strong culture. Instead of bringing the best of both worlds together, some people refused to accept the new culture and outwardly spoke against it, and even made fun of it. This type of reaction can cause conflict and limit what is within your own control. I made an effort to embrace the new culture and openly speak about the opportunities in front of us. After a while, if there was still negativity, I took control by avoiding any unnecessary interaction with the cynics.

It was possible to bring over pieces of the old culture that worked, but only after we accepted the new culture and were open enough to adapt. I saw many people leave the company. Some left on their own, while others were caught up in redundant positions and asked to leave. This was not easy to watch. However, many were left in a state of shock and felt as though they lacked control over their destiny. The unknown and unpredictability were scary, and we truly did not know where we would all land. However, we could control the small sphere around us. We could control our effort, or ability to assert ourselves within the new company culture, and keep the best pieces of our business moving forward.

I came to the realization that the old company would not have survived without the acquisition. Although I, too, was loyal and knew we did many things right, I believe I adapted to the new company culture sooner than many others. There were many people from my past in the old company who I felt had held me back or had not given me an objective chance to succeed (perceived or real). Many of these individuals were no longer with the company, either by their own choice or through the new company direction. What did I have to lose? While some others were waiting for instructions, I found myself jumping in with both feet. I decided that I would give it a try and move on if I didn't like it.

The openness to adapt was a boost in my own confidence because I knew that it was one of the things I could control. I started to enjoy it and stopped thinking about what negative things could potentially happen to me. I started thinking instead about the opportunities I could make for myself. I was controlling my attitude. I was having fun being in this unknown, non-prescribed new world. I was controlling my actions. I had new people listening to my ideas and opinions. I was starting to enjoy this clean slate, and felt like I was making a name for myself more than I had in the previous sixteen years.

As the full transition and buy-out was completed, I still saw people holding back and waiting for the next move to be made for them. Almost four years later, I still had conversations with people from the old organization who were still clinging to old habits and laughing at the new company culture. It was almost sad to watch because it was predictable that their success had reached its peak. My message wasn't about full conformance; it was about belief in a new company that we now all worked for together. Hanging on to the old was not controlling what they could control. It would only hold them back.

I remember a conversation with an executive from the old company with whom I had worked on and off for many years. He commented on how he planned to stay low and do just enough to get by after the acquisition. His premise was that it was easy to get lost in a company that large and he could just hold on tight. I felt as if he had lost control of many things he could influence. He minimized his ability to control his attitude, his ability to lead, and his ability to make a difference. Several years later, he maintained this attitude, and he was let go. That was unfortunate.

In the midst of what could have been a disastrous buyout of my old company and my potential long-term career, I found confidence and success because I took control of the things I could control.

18.

Show Compassion

In over twenty years of full-time employment, I have only called out sick two or three times. Early in my career in managing people, I would often comment on why the same people were always on the verge of being placed on corrective action for tardiness or illness. Each time someone called out, I had a cynical response assuming that there was some lack of truth behind why they called out.

I only thought in terms of what stage of life I was in at the time. Prior to being married and having kids, I didn't understand why people couldn't make arrangements to have someone else watch their children. When I got married, I was lucky enough to have a wife who stayed home and dedicated herself to raising our family. Why couldn't their spouse take care of their children? I still had a one-sided view. When my kids were born, I was back to work in a week while other fathers were looking for twelve weeks. When I worked forty-five hours, fifty hours, and sixty hours per week, I didn't understand why people couldn't commit themselves to those same hours. I didn't get it. I lacked the compassion and understanding of what others might be going through.

As part of my progress toward transformation, I began to have 'personal' meetings with my managers. I would periodically set up time and just talk about their families, interests, and hobbies. During these meetings, although it started off very hard for me, I refused to discuss business. I began to learn what motivated people and made them tick. I began to understand the passion people had for things outside of work. At the time, my passion was work. My passion, loyalty, and commitment to my company was the same passion, loyalty, and commitment many people had for their families, hobbies, and other things outside of work. I was beginning to understand.

I ran into someone I used to work with about five years earlier. He had moved to another state. He was still with the company and was

Show Compassion

visiting our office. We talked about the years when we had put in mind-numbing hours of overtime. I asked him if anyone even remembered that we had put in those hours. We both laughed because we knew the answer was no, and realized that much of it at the time was for non-productive show. The funny thing was that many of the leaders we were so emphatic about impressing were no longer even with the company. What we did remember was the fun we had, the people we touched, and the relationships we built—in simple terms, the things we *should* care about. When compassion is clear, the job will find a way to get done.

I think it sunk in when I sent an email to one of my direct reports. She was not in the office when one of her people called in sick, so I took the call. My previous cynical side of me would have questioned it. After I hung up, in the past, I'm sure I would have made up in my head the "real" story about why she had called out. Instead, I sent a short and simple email to her manager that read, "Penny's horse died. I finally understand."

19.

Set an Example

Be the person you want others to be. This is easy to say but hard to do. Whether we like it or not, in the professional world we are constantly on stage in plain view of people around us. Whether it is the people we work with, work for, or customers we serve, we are always being observed and judged—in person, on the phone, or through written communications. We are constantly being viewed, whether face to face, in conference calls, video conference calls, or just walking down the hall.

Observers are making judgments constantly, and we are being labeled with an ongoing reputation, good or bad, everyday. There is a laundry list of people with reputations in any office, and we have probably worked with them all at one point or other. In some cases, I know I've made my own uninformed observations and judgments of others.

Every company has one of the following: the complainer; the individual who refuses to work unless given A to Z instructions; the person who freezes under pressure; the one too good to associate with others; the one only in it for himself, and at least one overly competitive team member. The list can go on and on, but you get the point. Reputations and judgments can be made quickly and are tough to get rid of. There are traits and personalities that only add to the intensity of the reputations that bubble to the top. In any case, you are constantly being looked at and judged in the eyes of your peers and colleagues.

When our corporate culture was a little looser with expenses and entertainment, we had month-long events in one of our departments. We had contests and practical jokes, all in the supposed context of fun and employee satisfaction. Points could be accumulated as part of the team competition through practical jokes. The event culminated in a festive sports outing during which we went outside to release some tension and have some fun. I was constantly reminded by my manager that it was "supposed to" be fun. I say "supposed to" because over the years of this

Set an Example

annual event, the practical jokes got more intense as teams tried to outdo each other. Besides the risk of injury, there was a higher likelihood of risk to reputations if you were a target. The atmosphere began to get a cliquish feel to it, like the days of junior high and high school. The leadership encouraged it. As a manager, I was told to play along.

I like to have fun as much as the next person, but felt the intensity was reaching a level that was pushing the line of professional boundaries. As soon as I had this feeling, I could have done something. There were several examples I could have set. I could have had a long conversation with the leaders who condoned this and clearly stated what was on my mind. I could have reacted better to the jokes that were being played on me. I could have realized nobody was getting hurt and subsequently could have made it more of a team effort.

There were times I felt that I was individually being targeted, which only exacerbated the issue, pushing the jokes to see how much further our competitors could get under my skin. I would come in as early as possible to rid my office of whatever was in it or done to it. In the month-long event, I had a reputation for overreacting to the practical jokes, and I inadvertently created a game in which the other teams would see how much they had to do to keep me from cleaning up their practical jokes before everyone came in to work that day. This caused stress personally and created a divide in an event that was originally intended for the cohesion of the collective group. What kind of example was I setting?

I should have shown more maturity, gotten the right people involved, and set the example. I could have gathered the opinions of the team and determined how they wanted to handle the entire event. If we had talked through it, we may have even found that no one wanted to do any of it, but felt the peer pressure to keep it going. I had the opportunity to set the right example but never chose to take it.

Unfortunately, some of the events brought Human Resources into the picture that forced a long conversation with me. I had a chance to state all of my points. It was not easy or comfortable. However, it felt right. I wish I had set the example and not waited for HR to intervene. Although I moved on to another area the next year, the event was significantly toned down, and the pressure to find the next great practical joke was gone. Instead, it was back to good old-fashioned office fun, with competitions and food. By the way, you can never go wrong in making people happy with food.

20.

Do Something With Book Recommendations

I was stressed around the December holidays one year. My manager and I were not getting along well. We were having an especially difficult time communicating with each other. Still, the holidays are a time to reflect upon the previous year and to add hope for the coming year. I came back to my desk to find a small wrapped present from my boss. I opened it up and found the book, *Don't Sweat the Small Stuff*, by Richard Carlson. We did not have to communicate directly to understand the message he was sending me.

We were not enjoying the work atmosphere because we were creating an up-tight environment ourselves. We were also spreading this throughout the work environment. The subtitle to that book is, "And it is all small stuff." I got the point my manager was trying to say in a not-so-subtle way, and I really got hooked on what Dr. Carlson was trying to say. I received the book in 1997, and it has not left my desk since. I added a recurring calendar appointment to read a passage each day.

Reading a small passage everyday sets up my attitude with a fresh perspective and gives me the settling feeling I need to take on the business world. I am appreciative of the gift and the creative way my manager sought to provide me with the message he thought I needed. We still had our struggles and eventually found that we were both better off in other areas. However, my ability to tolerate my existing situation has improved with the enlightenment of the book.

Sometimes, a gift is just a gift. However, when it comes to book recommendations, especially obvious ones landing on your lap, it deserves to be read. Whether a book is a gift or someone says, "You ought to read this book...," take notice and add it to your reading list.

Even if the message is not as obvious, you should take notice. You may be in a class and a book gets mentioned. Write it down and at least read the summary to pique your interest. Your world can be broadened and diversified. If you have a tendency to think one way or have a strong perspective on a subject, have a willingness to see the other side. Your openness to try to get a different perspective than your own will broaden your ability to be more diverse in your thoughts and beliefs.

You should also consider different genres, different styles, and mix between professional and personal reading. You do not have to load yourself up with 365 days of pure leadership and business self-help books. A few summers ago, I challenged myself to read *War and Peace* for the simple sake of saying I could do it. I had stared at the book on the shelf for so many years. Coincidently, I am friends with a couple who were also in the middle of reading it. I was excited to be able to share their thoughts when we got together. We had a great discussion for about the first half of the book. The second half may take a little longer since they decided not to finish it. I won't give you my book review, but enjoyed the challenge of such a difficult and lengthy read. I tried to understand the complexity of the author's attempt to weave in so many characters, and I tried to understand what had gone into making it a classic. I laughed when I had heard that the author was paid per word. I now understood, at least, a little behind the making of a classic.

I had a great manager who was also my sounding board after we went on to other positions. He is now a good friend and he referred a book to me that he was very excited about. My manager friend had such a cool head in the middle of a crisis. He always maintained a level head and provided feedback when you didn't even realize it. He made the people around him feel these "aha" moments on their own—after a little prompting to encourage them to learn along with him, of course.

He was once described to me as having the ability to rip off your skin, and gently put it back on you. This so-called compliment of him was an accurate description because I was usually kicking myself after saying to myself, "How did I miss the obvious?" The book he recommended to me was *It's Called Work for a Reason: Your Success is Your Own Damn Fault*, by Larry Winget. My manager friend was always teaching me about taking ownership. He encouraged me to put myself into situations I had always wanted to be in, but may not have been confident in my ability to do it. The book he recommended was not my natural style, but was a good lesson in learning how to read something from a different perspective. I finished the book, inspired to take on the world—with a little chuckle, of course.

Many people have referred leadership books to me over the years, with some being better than others. Without getting political, I really enjoyed Rudy Giuliani's book *Leadership*. September 11 was hard hitting

The Transformation of a Doubting Thomas

for the United States and much of the world. Whether we liked it or not, Rudy Giuliani was the leader when one of the more tragic historical events of the U.S. occurred. He had several key messages including "surround yourself with great people" and "weddings discretionary, funerals mandatory." I enjoyed the cut-to-the-basics approach of his message.

If someone thinks enough of you to hand you, send you, or suggest a book, take advantage of it. You should be honored and humbled that someone thought of you when he or she picked it up. You should invest the time to read it and understand the connection that made it relevant to you. Your ability to like or dislike the book to some extent is irrelevant. The message someone is sending to you could be strong. The investment from you, and the possibility that you walk away learning something, is strong. Take advantage of the situation and read the book. Be aware: sometimes, there is not necessarily a connection to you and it is just a good book. There is nothing wrong with that, either.

21.

Live in the Present

I was always worried about what people thought of me, especially if I had made a mistake in the past. This may have held me back because I was worried about old perceptions people may have had of me. My concerns about whether someone liked me or not, respected me or not, or trusted me or not, impacted my confidence level and my ability to enjoy the job I was doing in the present. For the most part, I was impacting my own ability to do the work I loved to do.

I have had some bad days, like everyone else. I also had a few undesirable jobs that I needed to grind through. Unfortunately, these negative feelings and bad days had a tendency to linger with me, because I was worried about repeating a mistake or trying to over-impress someone with whom I wanted to make an impact. I am hard pressed to come up with immediate memories of truly enjoying what I had going on around me until the latter part of my career. The potential of repeating past mistakes worried me while my obsessive concern over potential roadblocks or traps kept me from enjoying what was happening then and there.

I think I was constantly trying to stay a couple of steps ahead of my next action, in an attempt to avoid past mistakes. I was living too far into the future at times based on my feelings from the past. I was too preoccupied to stop and live in the present. People around me were promoted and I congratulated them on their success. I would dig in, internally frustrated, and immediately went on to the next thing that needed to be checked off my list. I had presentations that went well but I never appreciated those successes because I was already thinking about the next big project that was due.

In the spring of 2010, I advanced through the first three levels of competition to reach my first Toastmasters District Finals. The winner of this Toastmaster's contest would represent District 45 (New Brunswick, Prince Edward Island, Nova Scotia, and all of Vermont, New Hampshire,

The Transformation of a Doubting Thomas

and Maine) as the Toastmasters International Speech Champion, and would then move on to the World Semi-finals. Only eighty-one people in the world would advance. On the morning before the biggest speech of my life, I ran into Joey Grondin. I recognized him from the 2009 fall conference, in which he'd given a presentation on "Developing Your Signature." His message was clear: be yourself and enjoy what you are doing right now. I told him how memorable that presentation was and how I'd incorporated some of it in my speeches, including the one I planned to do in the competition that night.

Joe was gracious and relaxed. He was conversational and engaged in our conversation. He saw my excitement and nervousness as a competitor, yet he did not even mention that he was also participating in the contest. He simply wished me luck and tried to provide me encouragement. Since he was a trainer in the previous fall conference, it never dawned on me that he would be competing.

He chose to avoid ruining my excitement until I actually asked him the question. He was allowing me to enjoy the moment and he was along for the ride. The smile on his face never wavered. Later in the day, I was nervously trying to calm myself down when I asked him what he did to calm his nerves. He said, "Enjoy the moment and live in the present." He also mentioned this in his book, *Living in Harmony with Our Children*. That day, he said to me (paraphrased), "You have done everything you can to prepare for this. Watch the audience and feed off their laughter and reactions. You will never be at that moment on stage to give this speech again, so enjoy it because it will be gone." Joe went on to win that competition, and subsequently the semi-finals, which put him in the top nine in the world. I found out later that he had been at the district level many times before and had never won. I was proud to watch his winning performance.

I was happy with my speech, after a small hiccup. I stumbled when I almost repeated a line, but that moment isn't what I remember most about my performance. I don't recall being nervous when I was actually doing the speech, but I do remember how excited and animated I felt up on stage. I also clearly remember the looks on the faces of much of the audience. It was the best time I ever had giving a speech.

The key is to learn from your mistakes of the past, but don't dwell on them or let them weigh you down. The past is over, so move on. You can also spend too much time worrying about what lies ahead as you try to predict the future. Will I fail? What will happen next? You only have so much control over any of it, and besides, there is a good chance it will change or not be exactly as you predicted anyway. Move your present

Live in the Present

forward by learning from the past, but see the joy in what you have at the moment.

Unfortunately, I also want to add that it can be over in a flash. While I was writing this passage today, I was on vacation but thought I would check my work email. I found out that there was a horrific auto accident near one of our East Coast offices. Two managers were returning from lunch when they were involved in a crash that killed one of them and put the other on life support. In cases like this, we can only love our family more than ever and give our thoughts and prayers to their families. The timing of the news was purely coincidental, but it is a stark reminder to hold on to the precious present moments while we can.

22.

Work Smarter, Not Harder

I have known too many people who work far too many unproductive, long hours. They cause stress for themselves while running in circles to get their jobs done. Working more hours and adding more effort does not always complete the task you are attempting. I have found that when I am running on a treadmill harder, it does not get me to the destination any sooner. As I have worked harder, I have often lost my ability to think with a level head and I start to build up that feeling of self-induced pressure, pushing me to work even harder.

We may think that working harder means putting on the blinders and looking straight ahead to get to the finish line. We also think this means we need to work faster and put in more hours to get more done. When the feeling of control continues to get lost, you may feel the need to work even harder as the pressure grows more intense to meet approaching deadlines and get to that finish line. The feeling you have in the pit of your stomach may tell you to dig deeper and get more intense. I suggest the counterintuitive advice of stopping what you are doing at the moment and regrouping. I recommend trying to understand the goal or the task you are trying to accomplish. Are you trying for quantity or quality, or both? Are you trying to meet a deadline, or just trying to get through your emails? Who is putting the line in the sand? Is it your boss or personal pressure you are putting yourself under?

Taking the time to stop and understand the true purpose of your mission and task is time well invested, which will assist you in coming up with a game plan and pointing you in the right direction. You need to incorporate what should be considered a lower priority and push that to the side for now, or delegate those tasks while you accomplish the most pressing task. These first steps are critical in order to see what is on the horizon. The ability to stop what you are doing to outline the next steps will save you time and effort in the long run. It is possibly the hardest thing for go-getters to do because we have been programmed to constantly be going a million miles per minute.

I personally like to maintain and reference things I have worked on in the past. I pride myself in organizing my working files (paper and virtual) for easy access and reference. Far too many people waste time reinventing the wheel. Are you always scrambling to put together a last-minute presentation? I have base slides that I constantly keep updated and put together. There are few times that I can just copy the slides in without making modifications, but it always gives me a starting point to get past the writer's block stage. It is also not plagiarism if you are copying from yourself and your team (as long as you have permission and are giving proper credit). The ability to have a solid foundation to work from actually gives you time to dedicate to the creative process (e.g., brainstorming, team discussions). You might be surprised that your end product looks nothing like the original, but that jumpstart puts it in motion. I have been around many hard working and smart people who have already put the effort into creating reference materials that can, and should, be used more than once when it makes sense. Using their materials is the sincerest form of flattery. The key is to keep it organized and updated, and know where to go to get off to a quick start.

There are certain times when there is a legitimate need to put in more hours to complete a job. You must ask yourself, is it necessary each day and each week? Do you find yourself constantly putting out fires and not being able to manage your calendar because of it? If this is the case, you should complete a self-assessment around what kinds of fires you are constantly putting out and what commonalities there are.

For example, at the end of every month is your manager asking for the same types of reports or summaries? The first couple of months may still be fire drills, but the rest should be routine. You should do what you can to build routines that minimize the unexpected.

In your preparation for the unexpected, you should categorize and target your efforts so that when you are under pressure, you know how to utilize your resources. For example, can you never find a phone number? If this is the case, make sure your phone directory is always updated. A few years ago, when we used to do more paper filing, I had a manager who tried to hide her files from me in a large drawer. When I asked her why she just didn't file them immediately when she was ready to put them away, she said it would take too long. Looking at her pile, it was true, but if she had done it right away it would not have been an issue. I realize these examples are over-simplified, but that is the point. The simple actions of doing things right away are often our biggest timesavers.

The Transformation of a Doubting Thomas

Don't let the simple tasks be your time constrainers. If you are not good at remembering to keep your directory updated, place a recurring appointment in your calendar as a reminder, delegate it to someone who can, or know where to get it from someone else. You can be creative in your simplicity, just make sure it gets done. Do not allow the small tasks to add up to a point where they are causing the frustration, or make you work harder than you need to.

Can you never find the notes you took from that meeting last week? Centralize them. Whether your notes are handwritten or done online, have an organized place to go back to them—you can have paper files, online folders, or scanned objects. It is not possible to remember every conversation you had. However, if you took notes, it was obviously important enough for you to jot it down. The key message here is to know where to go to get it. Do not dump it into a generic folder or stack in the inbox. To state the obvious, if it is related to something from Human Resources (HR), create a folder for HR. Your filing and organizational techniques will never be the same as anyone else's. That's all right as long as you know where to find things. I have seen too many "Miscellaneous" folders that only cause more hard work in the effort to find something that can be so easy to reference with a small investment of time.

Finally, set aside specific times to get to your routine tasks, such as reading your emails. You should set aside specified time to do this every day as opposed to managing them throughout the day while you are multitasking. Although some multitasking is necessary and can be done productively in today's busy world, such as eliminating junk emails during a conference call, attempts to run your entire day doing multiple things at once is not working smart.

If you are attempting to read critical email details during a conference call, you are not truly listening to what the other person is saying. In reality, you are not even multitasking since you are sacrificing one of the tasks. You are simply taking up a phone line while reading emails. I am being realistic and want to make sure we all have the appropriate prioritization and dedication to the task. Remember, it is not about just getting the job done, it is about getting the job done right. You may create more work than expected if you give a half answer to a conversation you were only half paying attention to, or erroneously respond to an email without reading all the way to the bottom. I know we have been told to do more with less and to keep our noses to the grindstone. I get it. Just be smart about it.

23.
Let Your Music Out

How often have you said one of the following: "I wish I could learn more about a different part of the business," or, "I wish I could learn to lead like the person down the hall," or, "I wish I could communicate more effectively," or, "I wish I could do something I have always dreamed of doing?" We often wish we could do more of something or start to do something we've always wanted to do. We may say that we do not have the time, the resources, or the drive to make it happen. We may say we have other obligations and priorities. What we don't have is the drive or commitment to take that one step it requires to face our "wish" head-on and make it a reality. We still have the music in us.

Oliver Wendell Holmes once said, "Many people die with their music still in them. Why is this so? Too often it is because they are always getting ready to live. Before they know it, time runs out." I say, "Or you can be hit by a bus tomorrow." It's time we let the music out, now.

Many of you have heard about the sad story of the Orlando Florida Sea World trainer, Dawn Brancheau who was drowned tragically by a killer whale in February of 2010. There has been controversy over the event. I will not go into the debate about animal training and the event itself. However, one thing is clear from the many pictures of her smiling with the orca whales. She loved what she was doing and died doing what she wanted to do. Her music was being played every day she was with those beautiful animals.

On a personal note, I learned the first twelve notes from the song "The Rose" by Bette Midler when I was about ten years old in school during music class. I have never forgotten how to play it. I never learned to play an instrument or even to read music growing up. However, for more than thirty years, I played these same notes on every piano I walked past. I have been an admirer of Elton John's and Billy Joel's music for as long as I can remember and I love the sound a piano makes, but I never learned

The Transformation of a Doubting Thomas

to play. At the age of thirty-eight, I got a call from my in-laws, who were eight hours into their twelve-hour trip to see us. I was told to get some help because they had a trailer with their old upright piano on it. What a nice surprise. We had hoped to get their piano when they got a new one, but could never come up with the right timing or means to move it from Maryland to Maine.

The next day, slightly sore, I began to "let the music out," literally in this case. I started with my wife's piano books, which I found in the piano bench from when she was eight years old. I began the journey to learn to read music and play the piano. I had my first informal recital in front of a close group of friends four months later on New Year's Eve. I do not claim to be great, but I do claim that I really enjoy playing. I also claim to be doing something I've always wanted to do. My three beautiful children decided they also wanted to learn to play. A couple of them stopped after a few years of lessons, but only to pursue other interests to let out their own music. I chuckle to myself when the two who are no longer playing walk by the piano and play a few notes of a song they learned. It's funny how you let out your own music and you start to influence people around you.

I share this personal story because it carried over into my professional work. I have found commonalities with people I never knew played instruments, and have come to work humming tunes I was playing the night before. My increase in personal satisfaction has bled into the professional work as I started each new day.

On the professional side, I felt I had things bottled up inside me. I knew I needed to communicate more effectively if I wanted to move forward with my career. I joined Toastmasters. Toastmasters gave me the platform to significantly increase my confidence as well as the ability to think more quickly on my feet, and to tell my stories with more personality. Toastmasters encouraged me to strive to go farther in the organization through communication and leadership certification. They walked me head on into the competitive world of speaking. Over the years, that has opened so many doors that I feel my own music had just begun to play. This book would not be possible if I had not won a door prize at one of the Toastmaster International conferences. I won a CD and book from a professional speaker who was present at the conference. I decided the next week after reading the book and listening to the CD that I wanted to do what he had done. I had always had these crazy ideas running in my head about wanting to write a book. I had work to do, but I wanted to let the music out.

We may not even know what music we want to play yet. We "don't

Let Your Music Out

know what we don't know," and thus may need to continue to search for our own music. When something gets your attention and you say, "I wish…" you should stop and ask if it is something you should pursue. You might surprise yourself by taking the first step.

24.

Open the Gift of Feedback

I loved feedback when it emphasized my strengths. I listened to opportunities I needed to work on. However, I never proactively sought out the feedback that would make me better, nor did I spend a lot of time after it was given taking action based on that feedback. I either felt the feedback wasn't valuable or I felt I didn't need it. In many cases, even if it was valuable, I typically fell back into old habits and waited until the next performance appraisal to hear something similar.

As previously stated, I typically hit the statistical performance expectations, so I rarely invested the appropriate amount of time or effort into making a difference for myself. The irony is that the same feedback given to me caused a lot of my frustration. I felt that the management providing me the feedback must have been part of a conspiracy if different people wrote similar feedback about me. I just didn't get it. I now tell people that feedback is not about agreeing or disagreeing with what they've heard, it is about doing something with it. Whether or not it has validity, at that point in time someone deemed it worth mentioning, therefore something needs to be done about it.

Feedback is considered negative in most people's eyes. It is human nature to defend ourselves or feel that others are simply being judgmental. Feedback is a process designed to make us better. Your reaction to the process, and the feedback itself, is what will make us stronger. With addictive behavior, it is often said that admission is half the battle. Your ability to admit that you are not perfect is your first step toward being more open to feedback. Your strength will show when you are able to recognize the validity of that feedback and be accountable enough to do something about it. We should all take action on the constructive opinions designed to make us stronger. Someone invested the time and had the courage to provide it, and therefore we should do something about it. The key is to understand that we need to move away from the feeling that it is all negative and just grasp hold of the nuggets of wisdom sitting on our doorstep.

Do we need to implement every bit of feedback presented to us? No. However, we need to seriously listen to it and consider it. Again, it is not a matter of whether we agree or not, it is a matter that someone somewhere perceives something about you that needs to be addressed. It is worth the investment to pay attention to this gift.

As we open ourselves up to being more accepting of feedback, we should also go on the offensive. We should be proactive about asking for it and not wait for a prescribed time or place. Who said you had to wait until your year-end review to make yourself better? If you are even luckier and work with a company in which you are having monthly conversations, you should consider yourself blessed.

We should take advantage of every feedback opportunity and never let it go by without actively asking what we can do to be better. Once you get comfortable with asking, you will start to gain the trust needed to expand the feedback process, thus allowing more sincerity and depth to the overall conversation. That depth, in turn, makes each subsequent conversation more impactful. The proactive approach may surprise some of the people you work with early on, but it will eventually allow you to build a bond. In time, you will find that more people become open to it. Try to imagine that every day is a holiday with the free-for-all feedback right there for the taking.

I rarely have meetings with people I directly work with without asking what I can do for them and what I can do differently. I now thirst for feedback and gain respect from anyone who is willing to stop and provide it to me.

I am an active provider of unsolicited, balanced feedback. I know that I had hesitation as to my own receptiveness to feedback early on. I also realize that many of my colleagues are not in the habit of asking for feedback, especially if they do not work directly for me. I do what I can to position my coaching in a way that they are an active part of the process or can easily buy in to it. It's important to not let a coachable moment go, since it is a gift.

We sometimes rely on the formality of our specific manager or a specific time of the year to receive an evaluation of our performances. What we need to do is give people feedback whenever it is relevant, regardless of who reports to whom, and give it when it is still fresh in all of our minds. Immediacy is often lost otherwise, which impacts the benefit. As the one providing the feedback, I work to ensure that I am balanced in my approach, and that I gauge how the person may react, but to still make it

The Transformation of a Doubting Thomas

a point to provide it as soon as realistically possible. The key is to provide non-biased critical feedback that will make an individual stronger. I have actually gained many mentors by providing this type of teaching feedback. The responses I have received have been along the lines of, "I wish someone said that to me earlier in my career," or, "Thanks for telling me something I thought I didn't want to hear."

Whether you are the giver or the receiver, be honest and be direct (with a filter, if needed). I am not a big fan of the sandwich type of feedback by stating something positive, something that needs to be improved, and something positive again. The prescribed approach is too predictable and often comes across as insincere. If you are honest and forthright, you will build trust, respect, and credibility. To maximize the feedback process, make sure you attack the informal feedback channels to gather information. You can speak to your peers, as well as people that work for you and people for whom you work. In addition, you can talk with business partners whose paths you may cross but to whom you are not directly linked. The third-party, objective point of view is always valuable insight. Just be open to looking for it and doing something with it. Whether feedback is from up, down, or around, it is a gift.

25.

Step Away and Clear Your Head

If something is not working, you are having a mental block, or you are getting frustrated with a situation, step away and clear your head. Your ability to mentally get through these types of challenging times is an important skill. Part of the mastery of this skill is to know when to give yourself a break to refresh that fragile mental state. Even in times of high intensity and urgency, the ability to take a step back and refocus on the situation is important. You can choose to spin your wheels or take a breath.

How long you step away is up to you based on the immediacy of what is going on around you at the time. Even a minute to push your chair back and not look at your computer could be beneficial during crucial times. If you can afford it, take a couple of minutes to get some water, or even better, if timed right, get up to take a lunch break. It doesn't mean walking away from an important meeting or confrontation, unless it makes sense. You need to make an individual assessment of the situation prior to doing this. However, stepping away to clear the head is invested time that allows you to then come back with new energy and focus.

When you do choose to do it, you are not walking away from the problem. You are walking away for an answer and for a fresh perspective. Walking away can help soften some of the stress and create enough of a change in atmosphere to get the juices flowing again or calm you down from major frustration. I have had many days during which I drank a lot of water or twisted the chair around. There are other days when I have had to stick my tongue out at the computer, have a quick laugh at how immature I just was, and move on with the day.

We all need to take ourselves out of the root cause of a problem or frustration and understand the rejuvenation factor. What you choose to do to break free for that moment can be anything. If you can afford the luxury to read the news, listen to music, take a walk, or even go for a run, it is important to cause a significant enough disruption to your spinning wheels.

The Transformation of a Doubting Thomas

The break is important. I have found myself staring at a presentation and getting stuck on a particular page with writer's block. I have tried to force my way through it by trying to find the next magical words. The inability to think clearly always seemed to get worse as I tried harder. If I just consistently make an effort to recognize that walking away is an important part of the process, I am much better off.

Make it a habit to break up a day of meetings or calls, or just go outside for the fresh air. If possible, try to find a regular time in your work day to schedule time away from the office, or at least step away from your desk. I actually put it on my calendar to take a lunch or break. Whenever possible, I personally like to go for a run and break up the day. I am convinced that since I started doing this I have been more productive and have had more creativity in my day. I am not sluggish at the end of the day. I knew going running on many days would add extra time. However, the increased productivity and satisfaction level actually cut significantly into that extended time. I was getting more done in the same amount of time. I know the concept of stepping away is counterintuitive to the notion of putting our noses to the grindstone, but it is worth it.

26.

Be Aware That "Nobody is Not Trying"

I actually had someone say this to me after I made a disparaging comment under my breath about someone I believed was not giving their best. I realized the passive-aggressive comment was not professional, but I felt like I had done everything I could do and the person was not listening. What I realized was that that person's definition of working hard and my definition of working hard were different. The individual calming me down at the time slowly convinced me that no one wakes up in the morning and says, "Today, I will refuse to work hard and I will not try." He simply said, "Nobody is not trying."

I began to understand that discrepancy in what I wanted and what some people wanted to give. I wanted a top performer out of everyone. I needed to understand that everyone was giving their best and it was my job to work closely with the individuals to figure out what needed to be done to get them there. I felt obligated to maximize the effort and performance, and to drive greater consistency. As I learned over time, effort and performance are like opinions, and they will often differ.

Many times, the effort and performance can be sporadic in some individuals, while you watch the solid rocks of your teams perform day in and day out. If a consistent performer is struggling on that rare day, it typically becomes very obvious. As a leader, we should work with the person to understand the root cause of these short-term struggles and offer our support. Many times, there is no need to micro-manage a person like this. The attention given asking, "Are you all right," may be enough. Providing assistance may also be as easy as letting someone work through it on their own and letting them know you are there to help, if needed. Performance managers should not allow this to be the easy way out every time. However, if you know your people well enough, you will develop a good sense of when to interject and when to just check in. The message is to ensure that you are not blanketing everyone with the same type of feedback.

The Transformation of a Doubting Thomas

You can also never go wrong with extra encouragement. It is the individual's ability to cope and break through that may make the difference. Individuals respond to certain methods differently and how you have built the relationship is important. Please note that this does not have to be a manager-employee relationship. It can be peers we work with, in whom we have noticed a dip in performance.

The key is to understand what the root cause for the variation in performance is, and what we can do to fix it. It is important to understand as early in the given day as possible if you feel someone is not performing at his or her best. Neither of you want the whole day wasted. I have seen too many managers wait until the end of the day to say something because they didn't notice until the end-of-day statistics came out, or felt too busy to offer a simple encouraging word or tap someone on the shoulder and let them know they were there for support. In these cases, eight hours could have gone by causing a non-productive day that must now be written off. Even if the effort was there but the performance was not, the lack of attention during those troubled times may hurt the overall team, and may cause further frustration for the person and send them into a longer slump.

If I am dealing with a person who consistently struggles, I need to better understand what motivates the person, what his or her skill set is, and change the way I am working with them. If I have gone to the same well over and over, I need to ask what I can do differently. Notice that I said what "I" can do differently. I may bark the same instructions or use the same canned motivation to drive the person. If it is not working, I need to change. Creativity is important. I can't give up on them. I personally see it as my own failure if someone struggles with his or her performance, and it is my obligation to fix it. Early in my career, this perspective was because I thought I would be looked at negatively by upper management. As the years went on, I felt the challenge of breaking through with all performers and building each individual relationship as my own motivation.

I banged my head on the wall about a particular individual who seemed to not get it. His frustration level and constant low performance made it look like he wasn't trying. He simply froze when speaking with customers on the phone. He said he wanted to do well, but his efforts did not exhibit this. The individual said he felt that he wasn't getting answers to make him better and felt he lacked direction from me. I felt like I had invested far too much time with him and it was time to put my efforts elsewhere on the team. We were at an impasse. I knew I did not want to give up on him, but I felt I could not sacrifice the rest of the team for this individual. I almost did give up. I tried to get him into another department, and asked if he really wanted to be with the company.

I woke up one morning and said I was going back to basics. I decided to try a different tack. I started asking him more open ended questions. I know he mentioned that he wasn't getting enough direction from me, but I decided to provide him with even less. I needed his buy-in. I asked what he thought his issues were by asking him simpler questions. I had previously been too targeted with my questions, many of which were assumptive in nature. I assumed I knew the issue and thought I was providing remedies to my self-diagnosed symptoms. What I failed to accomplish was getting to the real root causes.

I began to ask if the struggles were in the phone conversations themselves. Was it the selling to our customers? Was it the computer system? I knew he may not be able to put his finger on it, but I could act as a detective to diagnose where to start—but only after I had his buy-in to be part of the solution.

It is easy to have the poor performer sit next to other top performers and say, "Do what I do." People learn at different paces and in different ways. Some like classroom learning, others like visual stimulation, while many just like to be thrown in and just start doing it themselves. We can't blanketly teach each person the same way. In that case, the two of us began to rearrange how the computer system looked on the screen. We put certain applications in the front that he seemed to reference more often and placed other applications in the background that he didn't use as much but could get to quickly, if needed.

We both had an immediate epiphany. He had been overwhelmed with his own system set-up. His frustration translated into mincing words with customers because he was worried about where to go next on the screen. This impacted his ability to sell the most suitable products to meet the customers' needs. This simple change in his screen set-up created an almost immediate superstar top performer. His confidence level climbed and he significantly exceeded his performance expectations. He was making a difference on the team and was quickly becoming a leader. He came from the verge of elimination to the top of the podium.

Each individual is unique and needs to be driven, inspired, and motivated differently. Each person's ability to try and succeed also varies and needs to be understood at an individual level. If you think someone is "not trying," take a different, creative approach. We need to be patient when someone is not performing, since some people break out of it more easily than others. I am now convinced that most people can do it with the right coaching, leadership, and support. I have learned

The Transformation of a Doubting Thomas

that I can't offer solutions until I can identify and fix the symptoms first. I realized I had to try to understand the cause first. The person may be having personal issues or may not be feeling well, but I am confident that he or she did not wake up and say, "Today I'm going to intentionally have a bad day."

27.

Don't Let People Leave Their Manager, or the Company

Compelling research shows that people most often leave their manager, not the company. I spent almost two years solely dedicated to researching the topic of employee retention. I served on a one-person task force with a mission to "fix the attrition problem" we were having in our department of over two thousand people. As a call center, high voluntary turnover is somewhat expected, but my research found far too many easy ways to keep people. I invested a significant amount of time with management in the ten different sites in which we worked at the time. The goal was to ensure that I understood the root causes, and they understood the potential countermeasures to retain their people. It was clear that some managers needed to truly understand how delicate their relationships were with the people they worked with and how easily we lost good people. As an immature manager in my earlier days, I could empathize with a lack of understanding to the criticality of a strong bond.

Sometimes, managers of the people on the front line who deal directly with customers, for example, look only at their immediate team. If someone leaves, it's no big deal—they will get someone new and move on. Outside of the investment expense and effort to retrain, however, we are at risk of losing the knowledge a person leaving had, and, worse, are allowing many of these great people to potentially move on to a competitor.

According to Leigh Branham in the book *The 7 Hidden Reasons Employees Leave*, he writes, "89% of managers said they believe that employees leave and stay mostly for the money. Yet, my own research, along with Saratoga Institute's surveys of almost 20,000 workers... and the research of dozens of other studies, reveal that actually 80 to 90 percent of employees leave for reasons related NOT to money, but to the job, the manager, the culture, or the work environment." Beverly Kaye

The Transformation of a Doubting Thomas

and Sharon Jordan-Evans stated in the book, *Love 'Em or Lose 'Em* that, "A 25-year-long Gallup Organization study based on interviews with 12-million workers at 7,000 companies also found that the relationship with a manager largely determines the length of an employee's stay." Both references clearly indicate how much impact a manager has on retaining an employee.

During my research, I found that employees typically don't leave over an event, but add up multiple "little" events prior to making the decision to go. An employee may claim she left over a performance appraisal score, but it was most likely just the straw that broke the camel's back. She was most likely formulating thoughts to leave long before that discussion. The decision to leave typically festers over time as people gradually change their thoughts of leaving into taking action. The time it takes varies from days to weeks to months, and is contingent on many factors, including the economy, presence of a reliable back-up plan, and the employee's tolerance level with what is going on.

The employee often disengages from work responsibilities, culture, and management. This disengagement time frame will vary based on the severity of what the employee is up against, both personally and professionally. The responsibility clearly resides with the manager to identify the warning signs as far in advance as possible prior to a person making the commitment to communicate his or her intentions to leave. Once that announcement is made, it is most likely too late to save them. This is a key factor in knowing the people you work with and knowing when to intervene.

The organization has the obligation to invest the time and make the effort to save people who want to be there (and are performing or have the potential to perform). They obviously were good enough to hire, and deserve the effort. Sometimes, the person may just be in the wrong position. How many managers are willing to invest the time to find the right fit in the company? As an inexperienced leader, I remember saying, "Who needs that person anyway?" The company does. I have heartburn every time I think of the number of potential people who left the company on my account. I don't think the number is too large, but anything more than zero is too many.

Once, a young woman said to me that she was having personal issues and needed to talk. I said that I would be glad to talk after I got back from my meeting. She said it was important, but I chose not to listen. When I got back from the meeting—which was not very important—the person quit, and I never heard from her again. She had been a consistent performer and needed someone to listen to her issues. I saw the obvious

Don't Let People Leave Their Manager, or the Company

sign but did not attach the appropriate urgency to it. I'm sure a couple of minutes could have saved her.

I vowed to never let that happen again. A couple of years later, I received a message that a woman who had worked for me for a short period of time had quit without notice. She had come in to let us know and had already left. I took a chance and ran down to the Human Resources office and found she was wrapping up with them. I asked for a couple of minutes with her—a couple of minutes I could not have bothered with years earlier, when I chose to ignore another pleading person. We spoke for a while. She was having personal issues at home and also felt she lacked the appropriate support at work, since she was only an average performer. I knew she could perform well if she was focused. I asked her to go home and commit to coming back the next day, and we would work out a plan together. The honest and mutually direct conversation built a bond that grew as time went on. She became a consistent performer and eventually moved on to another line of business in which she became a top performer. I see her in the halls every once in a while and I burst with pride. I am proud of her staying with the company for an additional twelve years and still going. I am proud that I refused to allow my stubbornness, at the time, to allow her to leave. She was good for the company then, and is great for the company now. I just didn't know how much at the time.

Whether it is moving the person to another area, moving them to another manager, or working on building the relationship between yourself or an employee, the tough part is being attentive enough to see the signs and courageous enough to take action to save them. It is too easy to say he or she is just having a bad day and we'll talk later or, worse, we'll get another good person. Before you say, "Oh, well, " you might want to first contact the people who need to invest in the recruiting to get them, the trainers who will teach them, and all of their new surrounding teammates who will invest time in bringing them up the learning curve. Make the effort to retain and save good people. The relationship between managers and employees is critical to everyone's success.

28.

Be Flexible and Adaptable

Built to Last is a book about eighteen "visionary companies." These admired companies were recognized for their ability to "prosper over long periods of time, through multiple product life cycles and multiple generations of active leaders." The authors, James Collins and Jerry Porras, wrote, "Indeed, all of the visionary companies in our study faced setbacks and made mistakes at some point during their lives…Yet… visionary companies display a remarkable *resiliency*, and ability to bounce back from adversity." Companies that failed to exhibit flexibility may have had short-term success, but lacked sustainability. I'm sure it's not hard to forget the dot-com era.

My father worked for Sears Roebuck & Company for over twenty-five years. I grew up with the story of the stability of a company that thrived in the retail business for many years. I remember growing up with my Christmas holidays revolving around the Sears catalog. I remember conversations with my father about the history of the catalog and how it was here to stay. I also remember how long they took to adapt to using credit cards outside their Sears card or making decisions to sell other brands besides their own. Their inability to change with the times and their insistence on sticking with tradition cost them profits and many people lost their jobs as business models changed in the 1970s and 1980s in the retail space. Their business model was caught up in tradition and lacked the flexibility to adapt with the times. Sears has since adapted in many ways, but they are in a much more competitive retail environment with the likes of Walmart, Target, and online retailers everywhere.

I personally have averaged about a year and a half per position since I've been employed, with the majority within the same company. I always wondered if people really wanted me or if they just wanted me to move away. I have come to the realization that it was a little of both, depending on where I was in my maturity, my job knowledge, and my ability to help

Be Flexible and Adaptable

the business. In my constant changing of positions, I always found my adaptability to be one of my strengths.

As a child growing up, my family moved out of state on eight occasions. My ability to integrate myself into a new environment grew easier over time—first in school, and then professionally. When someone recommended *The First 90 Days* by Michael Watkins, I was instantly hooked on the idea of how methodical Watkins's message was with respect to what needs to be accomplished when taking on a new role. According to Watkins, it is important to "promote yourself," "accelerate your learning," "secure early wins," and many other key tenets. I realized that I was forced to transition so many times in my life that I had gotten used to living in a flexible manner, but probably not in the most efficient or effective way. I liked having the reference at my fingertips, so I pinned the book description up in my office, which contains a "road map for creating your 90-day acceleration plan." I refer to it often when I need a clear plan of attack in a new role or a new assignment, which has been often. I have recommended this book to everyone I have known who was taking on a new job. The message in the book is clear as to how much a company and an individual can lose if the transition to a new job fails. The book emphasizes the acceleration needed to be nimble as you begin your new adventure.

It is sad but true that people come and go in any company. In smaller companies, there may be less movement between roles and positions over time. However, people move out of town, employees retire, some quit, some are laid off, and others are unfortunately fired. Being prepared for new situations is important for anyone's success.

As mentioned in the introduction, "Change is inevitable, growth is optional." How you react to the employee movement—the constant movement in some cases—can make or break your ability to grow professionally. You may grow despondent because you have lost close friends, you may be frozen because there is too much work to do, and you may get tired of teaching new people what needs to be done. All of these examples are the negative approaches to change. Your personal growth comes in your ability to transform yourself to meet the challenge head on.

As you begin to ebb and flow with the changes, you, too, will be seen as a go-to person in times of crisis and change. If you have close friends who may have left the company, you can seek out their assistance as outside mentors and seek their objective point of view. If there is too much work to do, put together the business case for more resources, find efficiency opportunities, and find effective ways to delegate and spread the work. If there is a constant influx of new hires, come up with a clear plan

The Transformation of a Doubting Thomas

of action to rotate the responsibilities, tighten up the training guides, and enjoy the fresh perspective staring you in the face.

I have been through multiple jobs, managers, company CEOs, and acquisitions. All were potentially traumatic events for me personally, and for the employees as a whole. I know for a fact that I have come out stronger because of them, and because I adapted my attitude as the events were happening. I am convinced that if any of these events occurred in my first five years, I would have reacted differently, including overreacting with a negative approach. You may have heard the phrase often said in business, "If you are not moving forward, you are moving backwards." You have a choice to keep going with the flow, or stay behind. Your ability to be flexible and adaptable is critical to your success.

29.

Have the Right Priorities and Set the Right Perspective

Ask yourself if what you are so worried about at this very moment is the highest priority? Priorities are funny things. There are differences between urgent and important matters. There are fires that have to be put out, and people are busy and stressed and have to get stuff done yesterday.

I worked with a manager peer once who was obsessed with what people were wearing to work. He was the unofficial dress code monitor. At the time, we had a dress guideline, and not necessarily a dress code. However, he managed his work environment with the unwritten code of men being required to wear ties. He kept bringing the same person into his office to address why he wore a sweater over his dress shirts as opposed to wearing a tie. He had this conversation many times with the same individual. The sweater guy either chose not to conform, could not afford to conform, or just didn't understand the feedback (I doubt this was the case). The person was dressed nicely, but was not dressed the way his manager felt he needed to be. The amount of time and energy spent on monitoring what was worn and the wasted conversations could have been targeted toward higher priority issues. For example, there were employee dissatisfaction concerns and morale issues caused by being micro-managed for lower priority things. The person he was hounding was a decent performer and could have done without this type of counseling. Sweater Guy had no desire to move up from where he was and was content with coming into work every day, apparently prepared to mentally torment his manager. The irony is that the dress code changed a few years later to casual dress, including jeans. Now the person who received the feedback is overdressed compared to his colleagues.

I once had a boss who gave me a goal to recruit and hire twenty people per month for our department. I lived in a somewhat sparsely populated area and recruiting was often difficult. My team managed to hire about

The Transformation of a Doubting Thomas

fifteen to eighteen highly qualified people per month and felt proud of our efforts. I realize the importance of goals and the need to exceed them. However, this particular goal was set because it was a nice round number, not because it mathematically met the business needs. Each month my pride would be crushed because I was a couple of people short.

The number twenty became my manager's priority, and he lost his perspective relating to the quality of the hires and the impact his aggressive goal would have on stealing recruits from other departments we worked with. I had to make marginal hires to meet the number. These couple of extra hires per month met the goal, but caused heartache for the trainers because of some borderline attitudes, marginal performance, and higher attrition that had to be dealt with.

As recruiters, we became overly competitive and were internally fighting to make sure we got a candidate that was breathing. The extra pressure we put on achieving our own goals soured our relationships with other recruiters and our HR partners. I wish I was strong enough at the time to set the appropriate priorities by setting the appropriate goal based on our actual business need and capacity. I also could have stood up to my manager by presenting these facts and ensuring he noticed the teamwork needed to accomplish the goal, and emphasized the quality of the people hired was first and foremost the top priority. I identified what our priorities were, but I needed to effectively communicate them to my manager.

Alternatively, one of my favorite managers was considered a leader in the industry in his field. He was bright, communicated effectively, and was clearly leading his team to many wins. He found out that his mother was dying and only had a few months to live. During those few months, I was amazed at his willingness to drop everything to ensure that her last days were happy. He flew her on a long journey to visit with family for the last time, and made many visits during work hours to her home and hospital—both were over an hour away. I instantly gained more respect for his ability to realize that the job would go on without him. He made himself available for urgent matters, but knew he would never get that time back with his mother. By making himself available for urgent matters but giving us a clear direction to keep the business moving, we knew he trusted us to get the job done and that he was there for us. His mother died with dignity and respect, and with the pride that she raised a great son. He had the right perspective to not just say that his family was important, but lead by example for all to see. He taught us to set the right priorities and to have the right perspective.

30.

Build a Network

Brian Uzzi and Shannon Dunlap tell an introductory story in their study in the Harvard Business Review article, "How to Build a Network," about the well known Paul Revere as an historic figure in America. They then ask the question about the reader's familiarity with William Dawes. Apparently, he and Paul Revere rode from Boston on April 18, 1775 in separate directions with the same goal of letting everyone know about the beginning of the Revolutionary War. I say apparently because I had no idea who William Dawes was. The point the authors were making was how much more effective Paul Revere was in his networking ability.

Our society and culture have a great willingness to socially network through Facebook, LinkedIn, texting, and many other means. We have exponential links to good friends and colleagues, and are even willing to connect with many people we barely know—and in many cases people we don't know at all. However, social networking has evolved into its own culture and comfort level for people of all ages. When it comes to networking within your own company, I have found an uncomfortable hesitation among the employee base. We are willing to socially network with virtually millions, but we do not go beyond our own boss or our boss's boss when it could help our career immensely.

When discussing and presenting networking, I often ask how many are in mentor relationships. I usually get a decent response. When I ask the question, "How many of you have met with your mentor within the last month?" most hands go down. I think we feel the comfort of saying we have mentors, but many of these relationships quickly become inactive or dormant. We should maximize all mentor relationships as a networking springboard. Specifically, we should not only be gleaning advice and learning during these sessions, but we should always be asking questions, such as, "Who do you think I can meet with to learn about (fill in any subject here)?" and, "Do you think (fill in leader's name) knows who

The Transformation of a Doubting Thomas

I am?" If you have a mentor, make it an active relationship and use it to build your network. Why can't we use the same tenacity for professional networking that we might with social networking?

I am not naïve enough to think that company employees do not sit around the water coolers and conference tables talking about people. Much of this conversation is comparing one person to another. Whether the judgments are performance based, potential based, or skills based, these conversations are happening daily all around us. This comment is not to make you paranoid about interacting with others or about being yourself. The comment is to make you realize that each day presents an opportunity for you to promote yourself in the eyes of the people making decisions. It does not mean doing cartwheels up and down the aisles to get someone's attention, but it should cause you to realize that you have a professional obligation to represent the company well, and also present yourself in a way in which you can be recognized and grow. First impressions are lasting. Lasting impressions may be all someone has when your name comes up in a conversation. The key message is to take a proactive approach to building your network and making others aware of what you have to offer.

During one of my mid-year conversations, my manager told me about a conversation that had taken place around a conference table when names were being discussed for future positions. She asked me, "How many of the fifteen leaders around the table did you know?" I thought I did well when I said I knew about twelve of them. She said, "That leaves three leaders you don't know." She then asked, "Of the twelve people you do know, do you truly know them, do you know of them, or do you just know their names?" I said I truly knew maybe half of them. Therefore, my revised number was six out of fifteen people who could adequately make decisions about my future. She said I had work to do.

We continued the conversation. She reversed the questions and asked, "How many around the table know you well enough to speak intelligently about you and what you've accomplished?" The number was embarrassingly low. She emphasized a point I already knew: I had work to do. I instantly built time into my calendar to meet with a senior leader once a month. Every time I have done this, I ask who else I should talk to, and every time I seem to get at least three more names. My list is long, but the effort is worth it and has been extremely beneficial in my growth. I received more calls from senior leaders in the first year of doing this than I had in the previous nineteen years.

My boss shared this story because she was almost burned herself. Her mentor was in on one of those conversations about future moves and my boss's name came up. When her name was mentioned, her immediate manager said nothing. An extremely bright and talented individual was about to have her moment in the sun dismissed either because the manager did not like her, was in a bad mood, was intimidated by her own peers, did not hear the question, or simply just because. We can continue with the excuses all day long, but the point is that none of us can leave all of our eggs in our manager's basket, even if we have the highest regard for that manager. The mentor stepped in and sang her praises. Do you know what your manager would say about you if he or she had a chance? Are you sure? If you do not know that answer, or you are not sure, get to know the answer. There should be no surprises (good or bad). Communicate with your manager…often. What if your manager called out sick that day? Make sure he or she is talking with others about you, too. It is all right to ask this question, if you have built a strong relationship.

You need to set the tone for yourself on these types of settings to significantly increase your control of your own career. Most people are not doing enough to network because they are unsure of the value or definition. Networking is not "kissing up," as some people like to put it. Networking is not even intentional job searching. Networking allows you to understand how to better maneuver through the complexity of the business and the culture by improving partnerships, building bridges, finding integration points, and sharing best practices. Additionally, networking is making you stronger in the eyes of the decision makers and leaders. Unfortunately, all of this takes time and energy. I have found that people begin this trek only after they see a potential job opening arise. By this time, it is often too late.

When I started my first job in which I had no one reporting to me, I enjoyed the freedom of being on my own—until I realized that I had limited power to influence unless I networked and built partnerships. My job was the task force to assess employee attrition. I had no choice but to see the value of networking to achieve my goals to retain more people. I had to hit the circuit and speak to as many managers and frontline people as possible to ensure that I understood their opinions and feelings. Networking was beginning to get fun. There were points of views I would have never come up with on my own. I needed networking, and together with the management team, business partners, and frontline associates in other areas of the company, we were making a collective dent in reducing people voluntarily leaving our company.

So, after you come to the realization that networking is beneficial, the natural question is, "How do you start a conversation with someone you don't know? They're going to think I am crazy. How do I start?" The

The Transformation of a Doubting Thomas

answer is simple. Be honest and straightforward. Explain what goal you want to accomplish in the meeting. The person you want to network with should understand if your goal is to learn a different part of the business, to meet someone new, to job shadow, or to job search. The reasons may vary, and all are good for your growth. The constant, however, is always coming back to building an exponentially expanding network—make sure this is clearly stated to the person with whom you are meeting. Networking, if done right, can and should work for you after the meeting has ended.

Two things made the difference for me when I first started networking. The first two people I spoke with told me to contact them in a few months to give them progress reports. I didn't believe them or think it was a real request. When that incredible but nagging boss of mine asked if I had followed up with them yet, I said that I had not. I called them both later that week, and found out they had truly meant it. When I did it, one of them said, "You made my day," while the other said that he was excited about my progress and had already heard about some of my successes. The second thing that made a difference for me was when I thanked one of the people I networked with for his time and told him how much I had learned. He stopped me and said "thank you" to me for investing time with them. He told me that he got just as excited meeting someone new and adding them to his contact list. In addition, he told me how excited he was to share his business story with others. One of my first network contacts said to this person, "You should talk to Tom at some point. I think he may have something to offer to you." He said, "I already did, and I hired him." I was not shopping for a job.

I now understand that the nature of one person talking to another is really one person talking to many others. It is funny how things work when you are proactive and assertive, and even push yourself outside your comfort level just a little bit. Dots quickly get connected and people in your network connect with people outside your network to become a part of it.

31.

Lead the Parade

In the early 1990s when the word "clueless" was popular and I was in my early days on the phones talking with customers, a peer of mine looked over at another teammate of ours and said, "Some people lead the parade, some people watch the parade, and some people don't even know there is a parade going on." His reference for this peer was the latter. He was saying the person was "clueless" in a descriptive manner, but he was right. The person came to work each day and many times we wouldn't have been surprised if he didn't know what day it was. He was in a constant fog, and seemed to let the world around pass him by. It was hard to describe, but the fog was not about attention to detail or intelligence. He seemed to come to work, do his job to the minimum (not coast, because that actually takes effort to slow down), and went home. Sometimes, I wondered if he even remembered coming to work after he left. His cluelessness could only be accurately described as not even knowing a parade was going on.

    I imagine in most corporate and professional settings, your colleagues, your management, and your customers depend on you to do your job well. However, it can be more than doing well at your own job. You can be the leader of the parade. Be a leader strong enough to motivate more people to get in the parade—regardless of your position in the company. You are surrounded by people who may be coasting along professionally hoping to do no more than the minimum. You have an opportunity to maximize your own performance and the performance of others.

    You can assist in leading the company by staying informed about your business, and sharing what you learn with the people around you. You can read and watch the news about industry updates, and overall national and global events. You should also stay informed with internal company news when it is available, to give you a good idea of what is

The Transformation of a Doubting Thomas

going on in your surroundings. These surroundings are not just the physical space; you should also be keeping up with current events, business relationships, organizational changes, personalities, styles, idea generation methodologies, meeting preferences, and routines.

You can be part of the parade by asking questions and being curious. You can take the lead by sharing the information you've gained with others. The information is great for your own learning and development. You become a leader when you share your own development with others and allow the information to keep on giving. You can share stories via email, or talk about interesting business information during down times rather than discussing the most recent sitcom or sports. These types of conversations can spur new ideas for your business. You can also add to the conversation by sharing your best practices. You might call this, "Have a clue, get a clue, and share the clue."

I have been involved in many meetings, especially conference calls, in which people were obviously not engaged. The disengaged population are often multitasking. Besides the people who readily admit they are multitasking (you would be surprised at the number of people who come right out and tell me), there are the people who don't say a word during the entire meeting, other than to say hello in the beginning and goodbye at the end. The multitaskers also are the obvious ones who say, "Huh?" or "Can you please repeat the question," when they hear their name directly. Some are bold enough to say, "Johnny and I were just instant messaging and I didn't catch all of that."

Ryan Buxton cited in 2009 a new study from the Proceedings of the National Academy of Sciences that found that multitasking may do more harm than good. The article states, "Multitaskers are more susceptible to memory interference by irrelevant details, according to the study." The effort to move from one topic to another and the exertion required to return where you were impacts the true retention of information gathering for multitaskers. I won't be a hypocrite and say that I have never done it. However, since I've limited my multitasking, I have found myself asking what just happened in a meeting much less than I had in the past. I will say that my concentration level and my engagement has grown substantially since I made a concerted effort to concentrate on one task, one meeting, and one conversation at a time. I became more knowledgeable about what was going on and could react and take action in the conversation. Much of my success can be attributed to my effort to reduce my multitasking. I found myself taking more of a leadership role in many phone calls than I previously would have as an inactive listener.

We all have the opportunity to step up and lead the parade at times when there are stale or unproductive meetings. Although it may be difficult at first, try to professionally disregard hierarchies during the times when no one is stepping up. What I mean by this is that leaders are born during a crisis, or when there is no clear roadmap to get there. Be proactive by creating the roadmap and developing solutions yourself if they are not clearly in front of you. In a meeting, this doesn't mean just taking over or dominating it. It means assisting with the meeting facilitation in order to achieve the purpose of that meeting. In some cases, the purpose itself is unclear. Start with questions of the audience pertaining to what they want to accomplish and massage that information until you find a clear direction. You can also lead by turning meetings into brainstorming sessions, in which you can ask open-ended questions and facilitate dialogue, as needed. Don't wait for someone else to do it—everybody's time is valuable and you are simply looking for that value.

If you are not leading the discussion, you can at least take an active interest in a meeting and be ready to answer questions, assist the dialogue, and offer ideas or suggestions. You are already invited to the meeting; you might as well make it productive. If you feel the meeting is not worth it or is unproductive, particularly if it is part of a long-standing series, speak up. There may be other people in the room or on the phone who feel the same way. I realize that this is easy to say, and tough to do. However, try it and you will start to gain a comfort level and see the true impact you can have. Your fellow employees will see that you are only looking out for everyone's precious time, and this should increase their respect for your courage.

We have all most likely worked at one time or another with people who were constantly late for or missed meetings, lost track of time, derailed conversations to fulfill their self-interests, waffled at decision time, or never made a decision. All of these situations and personalities can cause frustration, confusion, and relationship tension that grows over time. However, many times, these are just the people who don't know that the parade is going on around them and can't even hear the band playing. Next time you are in a meeting or on a conference call with several people, look around and actively listen. Ask yourself, "Who is leading the parade, who is in the parade, and who doesn't even know a parade is going on?" Then, choose to be one of the few to lead the parade.

32.

Be Sensitive to Multiple Generations in the Workplace

We always need to be careful generalizing our assumptions when it comes to assessing employees of different generations. For the first time in the corporate world, we have four generations working side by side. How we manage the diversity of each of these generations is important. I have been in too many situations when managers made a blanket statement to a team of people consisting of multiple generations, and expected the same outcomes. We have to be cautious to manage each individual person and situation. Are you sensitive enough to know if generational differences in your corporate workplace are causing concerns?

We need to lead differently than we have in the past. We need to have a deeper understanding of what may be going through an employee's head: what drives people, inspires people, motivates people, and frustrates people? At the same time, we must now seek to include how generations as a whole are perceived. Based on when people grew up, larger groups of individuals may react to circumstances and situations as a collective group differently. We have found that people of different generations are motivated differently, were reared by their parents differently, and grew up differently. These differences are what make us great. If we can capitalize on these differences, we can create a stronger bond through them and thereby create a stronger company.

We need to understand that we all grew up in different settings, locations, times, and cultures. My kids don't know what it is like to walk into a bank. They only know about ATMs and watching Mommy and Daddy doing their banking online. These differences impact our ability to translate information at different speeds. Have you ever peered over the shoulder of a teenager while they were at a computer and tried to read the hieroglyphics of his or her instant messages or texts? It is hard enough trying to relate, let alone trying to read this new language. I at least know that, among other things, "POS" stands for "parent over shoulder."

As a child of Generation X, I have become a parent with much more involvement in my children's activities than generations before me. I have friends whose children chose to live in their parent's home longer than past generations. We also have been part of a culture in which every child gets an at-bat in t-ball, and medals and certificates go to all participants just for showing up. There seems to be less emphasis on winning and losing earlier in children's lives today, and competition is a secondary priority. I have talked with many parents who simply want to provide their children with the confidence to try new and different things, in order to help them figure out what they want to do as adults. There is some irony to this upbringing because of the parental intervention.

This type of close supervision, guidance, and support creates differences in when and how these people mature in their lives, including entry into the work force. I have had parents call after interviews to see how their child did, or ask what decision I made. I even had a worker's daughter write me a note asking me not to fire her mom. I guess the parental involvement goes both ways. By the way, I had no intentions of firing the individual at the time, but she knew she was struggling and must have discussed it with her ten year old.

The intense conversations I had on my retention task force interacting with frontline people and managers of all generations helped me to understand what it took to retain them. The research provided me with plenty of factual and anecdotal information regarding managing various generations. The fact is that for the first time in any generation, many offices are filled with colleagues from the last four generations. We have the older generation (typically defined as people born before 1945), Baby Boomers (typically defined as people born in the mid-1940s to mid-1960s), Generation X (or the MTV generation—typically defined as people born between the mid-1960s to early 1980s), and Generation Y (typically defined as people born in the early 1980s or after).

We have situations in which people from the older generation are coming back into the work force from retirement due to boredom or financial necessity. How do you train and manage someone who truly knows they are working simply for a paycheck, and do not plan to climb the corporate ladder? Or, did I just make my own blanket assumption with that statement? I don't have the right to make the assumption that they don't want to climb the corporate ladder, or that they aren't just as driven as the twenty-two year old looking for the next manager's opening. We have to be careful of biases, and make no assumptions. What if the person has twenty years of management experience and their

The Transformation of a Doubting Thomas

current manager is twenty-five, with only a year or two of experience? The multiple generations add a new complexity to the work environment and add new layers of sensitivities required from managers and non-managers alike.

None of the situations described or questions asked are easy to address and answer. However, knowing that there is a potential need to adapt our style based on generational wants and needs will make us stronger leaders and more effective professional colleagues. Managing, or even just working next to, a returning retiree or a new hire straight out of high school doing the same job has to be handled based on each individual first and foremost, with a quick balanced glance into the overall generational consideration. Each person will have different goals, different experiences, and different expectations of the business and manager. Once we understand this and act on it appropriately, we will be ahead of the game.

Generation Y has been in a technologically fast world their entire lives—some seem like they were born with a cell phone in their hand. I have found that many Gen Y individuals are often looking for a fast-paced and flexible environment. A manager may have to go out of their way and be creative to keep someone from this generation occupied and moving. Gen Y is also known for constantly looking for positive and reinforcing feedback. When a manager screams at a Gen Y person for a small mistake, it may make a person who is always on the go and looking for constant stimulation simply not return the next day to work. The manager must assess the situation and may need to be prepared to invest a lot more of their time and effort to ensuring that they are keeping up that stimulation, providing the attention and praise that individual may be thirsting for.

A manager must also be flexible and understanding. I once had a young man call out "well" because of a new video game release. He spent over ten hours staring at a television screen and playing the game with no guilt in the world for missing work. He came in the next day exhausted and slightly unfocused. But he came in. He respected me enough to tell me the truth, and said he was taking the time afforded him by the benefits of the company. I think I would have kicked and screamed earlier in my career. I got a good chuckle and we went on with our day. That person went on to become a very successful technology expert in the company.

Baby Boomers are often identified as wanting to be defined by their job responsibilities. They value hard work and team work. Managers may need to be sensitive to putting them into more group-related functions, as opposed to assigning an independent task.

It is important to be careful not to stereotype. You should monitor

Be Sensitive to Multiple Generations in the Workplace

and communicate regularly to get a feel as to whether these blanket assessments are accurate to the individual with whom you are working, or if that was just generational bias statements observed by common employee researchers. As a manager, it is critical to make your own individual assessment, but understanding some commonalities within generations may be the start we need in order to have an effective conversation. We should use our own observations to see if any of these so-called tendencies are accurate while we get to know each of the people working with us. The key message is to understand whether any of these factors impacted our decisions and actions regarding work assignment, management style, and how to drive the team toward a collective goal. As a colleague in the middle of multiple generations, I can look to build bridges and find creative ways for the most effective collaboration, training techniques, and partnership among everyone.

We have had generations who supposedly always question authority and the status quo. We have labeled certain generations as being constant multitaskers, disciplinarians, and so on. Each generation has had different backgrounds and influences, and each generation has their own visions, opinions, and ideas. We must also remember that individuals also have their own visions, opinions, and ideas.

We need to be aware of the generational differences as a whole, and sit down with each individual to understand what their visions, opinions, and ideas are to weave together the tapestry of the team in order to make it stronger. You should consider generational groups' opinions on many facets in a work environment, such as:
- Flexibility—schedule, family situation, outside obligations
- General learning ability—fast learners, visual versus book
- Coaching—give direction and tell them to go do it versus hand holding
- Work/life balance expectations—weekends, nights, single parents
- Feedback and motivational style—constant encouragement, hands off, hand written encouraging notes, team functions

We must always seek to build trust among the various generations and gain mutual respect for each other's strengths. We must not make any assumptions or generalizations. We should be flexible in understanding everyone's backgrounds and individual contributions to maximize the strengths of one another, while using our generational knowledge as a tool to build relationships and glean an understanding of the person as a whole. The company, in turn, will be given the gift of balancing the workforce with all generations in order to get the best of all groups.

33.

Control Self-imposed Pressures

I remember too many times when someone asked me to get something done immediately for them. When that happened, I knocked down walls to get it done. I sometimes felt like a dog that had just picked up the morning paper and was waiting for my reward, only to often get passed by without an acknowledgement. I didn't understand that the word "immediate" had multiple interpretations. The requester might have given credit to someone else or didn't even remember who did it in the first place. I would put undue pressure on myself and then try to figure out what went wrong. Unfortunately, when receiving these types of requests, I often did not effectively ask for clarification or understand the expectations.

I found myself wondering why I always put this type of unnecessary pressure on myself, or find myself getting riled up when the end result did not come out the way I wanted it to. I tried to understand why I dropped everything else I was doing or poured my heart and soul into something only to realize later that it was a request in passing, or that it could have been done just as easily at a different time. I had to better assess the urgency and importance of these requests. I had to gain a better understanding of what needed to be done now versus later. I also should have compared what needed to be done for the business versus myself. Finally, I needed to understand whether I was putting the pressure on myself or if it was truly pressure about a pressing task that genuinely needed to be addressed quickly.

When I didn't get the attention I felt I deserved for accomplishing something, I would typically invest far too much time worrying about it. I might have been upset for thinking that a mistake was made and the requester didn't want to say anything. I searched for the proper credit when I felt it was due. I had to come to grips with myself. I needed to make the move to be more accepting of who I was and what I was doing—everything else would eventually take care of itself. I began to make an

Control Self-imposed Pressures

attempt to take the pressure off myself by concentrating on the quality of my work and just try to learn from the experience—good and bad.

Many people have a tendency to be harder on themselves than anyone else. The pressure to get the task done, the pressure we put on ourselves in the hope that it was done right and then waiting to see the reaction of others, all adds up. The question is, "Adds up to what?"

I have found myself in situations when I felt like I should kick myself because I said something stupid or forgot to ask a pertinent question in an important meeting. I found that I would drive myself crazy with these thoughts running through my mind, putting more and more pressure on myself to be perfect. I wanted to get everything done for *everyone* at the exact right times. I include myself when I say *everyone* because I was typically my own worst enemy.

I started to realize that many people have memories like a dog—they last a couple of minutes and move on. I worked with executives who were responsible for millions of dollars for the company and some who were responsible for hundreds and thousands of people. I began to realize that some people have more important things to do than remember a minor mistake I may have made. Even if the mistake was remembered, I found it important to ensure that everyone saw that I had learned from it. I was the one putting the pressure on myself—pressure that no one else was feeling.

I had to do a better job of ensuring I was clear with expectations relating to time frames and deliverables. There may be situations in which you do have to drop everything, or there is a flavor of the day that needs to be addressed. Sometimes, there really is a pressure to get something done. However, more often than not, I was doing my job well, exceeding my boss's expectations, and was just putting too much stress on myself. I needed to free my mind of this clutter and just concentrate on the job at hand. I also needed to do a better job ensuring I wasn't asking too much of myself.

I couldn't sleep last night. I yelled at my children because I could not concentrate on writing this book, and I felt guilty. Naturally, my reasoning for yelling at them was justified in my mind because it must have made sense that the paragraph I was working on was the most important thing in the world to me at the time. I know this is a ridiculous thought, because nothing is as important to me as my family, but at the time when my emotional pressure was high, I had to find some other silly reason as to why my children were at fault.

I began to assess the situation as I was tossing and turning in the night. I had set very aggressive and specific internal goals relating to this

The Transformation of a Doubting Thomas

book. I was meeting my own time frames and pacing it out appropriately according to my own expectations. There was no publisher on my back to get it done and there was no one forcing the issue except me. However, my internal goals were stressing me out and building up tension to the point that I was taking it out on the people I love.

I was forcing myself to wake up early to put my ideas and thoughts on paper as quickly as they came to me. I wanted certain sections written by certain times. I was forcing my own direction. It's good to be aggressive with goals, but there also needs to be a balance with everything around you. I was upset at myself for getting unnecessarily upset at my children. I had no intention of writing a passage about internal pressures, but I know how much each of us drives ourselves to succeed personally and professionally. We will succeed. However, we need to skim some of the pressure off the top that we ourselves have created. When I woke up the next morning, I did not log in to write my book, but I did apologize to my children and thanked them again for being my teachers.

I invested time to reevaluate my goals and decided to extend my own timeline a little longer to ensure that I was putting out a product I would be proud of. The reassessing of a timeline, or giving ourselves a break, does not mean being lax with deadlines, internal or external, and does not mean being less aggressive with respect to personal or professional goals. It means incorporating time to provide breaks and down time to stay fresh, and make sure we truly know what's important and urgent. Make sure we understand whether the pressure we are feeling is self-imposed. If it is, reassess whether or not those pressures are too intense and thus impacting the quality of the work we are producing.

We should also ask if we are on the same page as the individual requesting our time, even if we are the requester. You might be surprised at the number of instances when you are not in sync. Stop yourself in mid-action and ask what *needs* to be done and what you *want* to get done. Need and want will have a different urgency and importance attached to each. As you continue to regularly reassess the pressures, you will begin to assimilate to what is 'real' pressure and how much is self-imposed.

34.

Play Music in the Background

I am a huge fan of music. I enjoy many genres and have always enjoyed having it playing around me as much as possible. As the years have gone by, I have progressed from my first AM transistor radio with a one-ear primitive headset, to a clunky tape player I wore while mowing the lawn as a kid. My lifeguarding days in the summers were filled with the radio blasting and the swimmers around us all having a great time. I eventually put speakers in my office to play my CDs and transitioned to speakers for my MP3 player.

    I am not sure why it took so many years for me to get past the "unprofessional" hesitation to play music in my corporate environment. We have heard that "music soothes the savage beast." When I am grinding out the work on my own and am not in meetings or speaking to customers, I listen to my library of music. It calms my nerves, inspires me, motivates me, and just puts a smile on my face. I feel more in control and more alive when I am playing music softly in the background. Many times, I don't even realize what song is playing. Sometimes, I often mouth the words to songs I know well. I listen to many different types of music depending on my mood, or simply listen randomly. In most cases, it doesn't matter to me as long as there is music playing.

    I found over time that people would come into my office and hear a song they had not heard in years and make an engaging comment. The music became a conversation starter in some cases, or just personal memories for others. These conversations spurred a new event for a group of people I was working with. I started walking around the floor and would ask music trivia every day. This simple act had a positive influence on the team's overall morale. Even people who were not interested in music began to yell out answers, and surprised themselves when they knew more than they thought. We started to play music in the morning as people were coming into the office, and found that there was an official

The Transformation of a Doubting Thomas

One-Hit Wonder Day in September each year that we began to celebrate. In group settings, we tried to vary the mix of music to include the interests of everyone. We used it more in group celebrations, and played it lightly in the background while everyone worked throughout the day. I found that music as a motivational tool was as effective as anything else out there.

I like all kinds of music, although I realize that there are picky music critics out there. They may need rock to run and soothing music to work with. The point is not the music you choose, but that I have found the therapeutic advantages of music in my own professional career. Music allows me to put myself into a state of mind that is strong and helpful in my workplace.

When playing it by myself, I usually don't even realize I have it on in the background any more. What is interesting, however, is that I do notice when there is pure silence; I know I like the music to motivate me. I find myself tense until I press the play button. Maybe I just like the company of another voice. I am not sure of the reason why. I just know the difference it makes in my mindset as I am working through the day. If you can find a way to do it, give it a try.

35.

Do You Know Your Value Proposition?

I had a manager who constantly asked me, "What's the value proposition?" What she was really asking me was, "Why should I, or anyone else, listen to your proposal or opinion?" My responses to these questions were often, "Because it's the right thing to do," or, "Because it's my opinion," or many other generic reasons that missed the mark. I grew frustrated over time as I continued to develop the answers she sought. I would expand as time went on to include, "Because it saves us money." She would respond in a manner similar to, "So what?" or, "Why would the customer care?" I would expand to include customer impacts, and she would tack on questions relating to how I thought the people who needed to execute the plan would respond, or what would those funding it get out of it.

I was getting a lesson in ensuring that I was formulating a plan that took into consideration what was needed from people who had a stake in the game. I was also learning lessons in formulating a well-prepared plan that would get people's attention and create easier buy-in for implementation. I needed this manager's approach to teach me how to think things through so that I could present a compelling case that was easy to comprehend. I wanted to add this approach to my go-getter style. I charged forward full steam ahead to learn more.

I also needed to learn to consider unintended consequences. What might be good for a certain population may not always be good for the whole. How many times, as a customer, have you heard a service representative state, "Because that's our policy." To a customer, they are saying, "So what." The customer is not always right; I had to consider the question of the customer's impact on my own ideas because I didn't want them saying, "So what."

I remember far too many times when we created a new rule or process and simply wrote a memo, an email or posted it to the company website for the people who needed to execute it. We expected the employees

The Transformation of a Doubting Thomas

to simply embrace and implement the changes. The worst part, many times, was that we did it with very little input from the people who would be charged with doing the job each day. I can remember the times we did this and then had to retract it because we hadn't anticipated the downstream effects of our decisions.

My manager was not being cryptic when she asked me, "What's the value proposition?" She was just covering all bases. She needed to ensure that I had gained multiple perspectives and opinions, thought of various scenarios, and formulated the value attached to what I wanted to say. I began to think more holistically and was able to better articulate my points because she had a solid foundation. The value proposition methodology became an ironic lesson in itself. My own value was growing in the eyes of other leaders as she saw me implementing the feedback.

36.

Build Credibility and Success through Effective Communication

Communication is one of the most critical skills to have in any professional setting. I was in a planning session one day when the key speaker mentioned that "Ninety-eight percent of all problems in the world come from miscommunication." I've never been able to validate this statistic, but I also would never argue it, because there is truth to it. We could probably reassess many of our past issues and identify some root factor that came down to ineffective communication, whether it was due to poor listening skills, communication channel ineffectiveness, or over complication of directions. I got the point.

I thought I would share a true story as to why communication is important, as expressed by one of my daughters who was eight years old at the time. Please note that the names have been changed to protect the identity of those involved.

My daughter was given a note from a little boy named Adam asking her to "go out with him." The teacher saw the note and asked my daughter about it. She said she thought it came from Adam and that it had just been sitting on her desk. The teacher went to Adam and said, "Did you write this note?" He replied, "No." She asked Chris, a little boy who sat across from Adam, "Is this note from you?" Chris replied, "No." Now the teacher was confused. She said to Chris, "You don't know anything about this note?" Chris said, "I know about it." Now the teacher was a little annoyed and she said, "But I just asked if you wrote it and you said no." Chris said, "No, you asked if it was from me and it's not—it's from Adam." So the teacher said, "Adam, I asked if the note was from you and you said no." Adam said, "No, you asked if I wrote it. My handwriting isn't very good, so I had Chris write it for me."

Miscommunication is the root of too many problems. I cringed every six months when I read the communication sections of my performance

The Transformation of a Doubting Thomas

appraisals. I lost confidence over time with my own communication ability, whether it was written, verbal, interpersonal, small group, or business communications. I struggled managing up, managing down, and simply having effective conversations with peers. I knew I had the skills, but always seemed to struggle. I had difficulty in finding my communication style, and with determining who I wanted to be as a communicator and how I most effectively wanted to communicate. When I lost my confidence in communication, I had difficulty in believing I could ever succeed at my company. I couldn't identify a true communication style because I lacked the confidence to truly know myself or my capabilities. Let me share a performance appraisal quote relating to my own communication.

"Tom needs to be more concise with his communication style. He needs to ensure that he understands his audience and his ability to adapt based on who he is interacting with."

I did not adapt my communication style regardless of whether I was talking to a peer in the hall or whether I was communicating with senior management. I had significant opportunities to also be more clear and concise. I could have provided executive higher level overview, as opposed to stuffing every little detail into a presentation, including speaking notes directly in the main bullets on the slides. I now ask the following questions of myself ahead of time, "Who is the audience?," "What is the intended outcome of the meeting?," and "How much information do I think they will need?" These questions allow me to understand how much information to have on hand and what kind of preparation will be needed. For example, will I need to be surrounded by numbers and statistics, or will the audience trust the numbers on the page and want a directional recommendation? When asked questions, will the audience want a high level overview or a detailed storyline? I found that the feedback wasn't specific to making my responses shorter, the feedback was directed to having me be clear and succinct based on what a particular audience wanted. My ability to adapt to the audience needs won over many critics as I improved.

In another evaluation, it was recommended that I, "Ask questions to ensure a full understanding."

I wanted to be the person with all of the details and all of the answers. I was the first to answer questions, or the first to speak up. Often, if I was leading a conversation I would exhaust everything I knew prior to opening up the meeting for questions. I typically didn't even pause long enough to ensure that everyone understood what I was talking about. I often lost my audiences and they became frustrated. They frequently did not have a chance to speak, or lost interest because they could not follow the path I was taking them down. I also lost credibility because I could not generate buy-in to the ideas and concepts because they came across as my ideas alone. I now use silence as a tool. I generate conversation up front by asking open-ended questions to ensure that the audience understands and is engaged. I use pauses to create enough time for people to ask questions. If I am leading the conversation, I often stop to ensure clarity and elicit opinions along the way. I try to ensure that participation and buy-in is an ongoing part of the process versus a question at the end of, "Do you agree?" I found this style suits me better and has enabled me to be more effective. This way, I have found that I have to explain less and do not force myself into a position that inundates the audience with unnecessary details, because they are now an active part of the conversation.

"Position ideas with your audience in mind…need to be more confident in presentations to senior management; don't second guess self."

That feedback was a mouthful. Apparently, I didn't grasp the audience feedback when previously given and I needed it reinforced. As stated in the original piece of feedback, "Understand his audience," I needed to ask the right questions of myself ahead of time in order to formulate my ideas and learn how to most effectively get them across to the audience. These questions allowed me to better position my ideas based on who I was speaking to and allowed me to get creative in how to do that. As I became better accustomed to understanding audience needs, I gained confidence in my own abilities.

I had a key learning moment when I worked for a manager who emphasized taking the emotion out of discussions and stressed sticking to the facts. I tried to become more level headed as I answered questions and presented ideas. I was open to expanding on my ideas, but sold the merits of those ideas based on solid facts I'd gleaned from information I gathered from customers or people I worked with. I made my positions more holistic based on a collaboration of facts that allowed me to confidently present them to all types of audiences, based on the needs. My confidence went through the roof. I had the backing and support of actual results and verbatim information that solidified my overall position. I figured it out based on the obvious clues my audience was presenting to

The Transformation of a Doubting Thomas

me, such as, "I would not have thought of that until you presented the customers' point of view," or subtle clues like, "I think this is interesting information I would not have thought about until you mentioned it." I learned to not only present with facts, I learned how to read the audience to determine the appropriate amount of facts.

"Avoid shutting down when others don't agree with you."

I had another manager who told me it was all right to be challenged and to have a debate during these discussions. I was not the biggest fan of confrontation. I had not realized that "shutting down" was a form of communication until I realized it was my way of dealing with more difficult situations. I was providing my audience with details relating to non-verbal cues I was giving off in times when I did not agree. The silence was deafening when I did not agree with a point of view. I typically got defensive in my short and terse responses until I had exhausted all avenues, and then sat in silence fuming while others offered their dissenting opinions. I took their critical positions personally. I had to learn that they were not personal vendettas; it was just an attempt to hear all sides and make the subject palatable to as many people as possible, and more importantly, come up with the best solutions—even if they weren't mine. In some cases, I was simply being asked to clarify, but had stopped truly listening enough to be an active part of the conversation. I had to be a more engaged listener and ensure that I truly understood the other point of view. My root issue was not shutting down; my root issue was the listening. As soon as I became a better listener, I could formulate and articulate my thoughts and opinions more effectively.

I had several obstacles in accepting the communication feedback that I needed to get into my thick head before I would readily accept it. First, I didn't truly believe it early in my career. I was convinced that my communication diploma made me an effective communicator and that it did not have to be nurtured. Apparently, I missed the day of class that said learning communication is progressive and constantly evolving. Second, I was detail oriented. I convinced myself that my messaging was clear because of all the information and details I was providing. I felt the need to constantly repeat my points and inundate the audience with information until I felt they got it.

As stated previously, I talked myself into believing that many of my managers just read my past reviews and they were not accurately assessing me regarding my communication ability. I was not cocky or overconfident in my communication. I was losing whatever confidence I had every time I had to read my performance appraisals. I did something that was more difficult than waiting every six months to read it: I started to pull them out every two weeks. I knew I had a weakness, whether it was real or perceived, and I knew I had to address it head on. If someone thought it, I eventually convinced myself that I had to do something to improve it, and communication was the constant string that was being pulled through.

My turnaround came when I slowly started to be more active in the review process. I had managers who invested their time in building a relationship with me, who gave me the confidence to ask questions. I started to finally believe I could improve, if I just decided to take action. I started asking the question of anyone providing me communication feedback, "How?" I actively sought specifics and almost treated the feedback as a research project. I sought role models who exhibited skills and styles that worked, and I grew to enjoy the challenge of making myself a better communicator.

"How" to fix your communication woes will vary based on the individual. However, anytime feedback is given, the recipient has the right, and I would say obligation, to ask for an explanation and further detail of "how" to fix it if the individual providing the feedback fails to address it. What tangible actions can an individual take if they read feedback that simply starts with "You need to adapt...," or, "avoid...," or "position..."? The employee needs to make it a two-way conversation and get examples and explanations that give the context necessary to take action based on that feedback.

I had realized that the simplicity of asking the question, "How?" during a feedback session would make a significant difference in my ability to grasp hold of something to work with. For example, I wish someone could have told me twenty years ago that I could improve my communication confidence by joining Toastmasters International. My first year-end performance appraisal after I joined Toastmasters read, "Tom's organizational and communication skills are his key strengths." It was the first time I was not asked to improve something regarding my communication. I was learning the value of proactively taking a role in the feedback process and was beginning to understand that communication is a learned trait that needs to be nurtured. I was gaining confidence in my own communication ability. I started to realize the clear connection between confidence and communication. The combination equaled communication effectiveness. The communication effectiveness turned into greater credibility and success.

37.

Understand Communication Preferences

There are so many forms of communication in today's professional environment. Professional communication has evolved from a face-to-face, memo, or phone-driven form to so much more in today's business. The emergence of voice mail, email, instant messaging, video conference, and texting has changed how, when, and with whom we interact. The list will only continue to grow as new technologies emerge.

The dynamics of our interpersonal and small group discussions are impacted based on the communication preferences and choices people make. For example, our ability to more actively listen and be sensitive to voice cues is heightened when we are on the phone, versus being in person. Attention spans are also impacted by other factors. You can be on a conference call with twenty people, and a few participants have side conversations via instant messenger or email. Their attention and engagement are impacted, and may influence others around them. Other people may be conducting non-related business on the side that they see as a higher priority. Face-to-face meetings, and video conferencing to some extent, have their own communication influences brought about by non-verbal messaging by allowing the participants to see facial expressions and reactions.

The ability to type messages instantly also has its own pros and cons. The messages are typically short and concise. However, there is often a lack of context in the message which may force the need to have significant clarification back and forth. I have found outside of the many symbols being used to express our emotions during an instant text message interaction (emoticons), overreaction is brought into the text message interchange due to the immediacy of the channel. People have a tendency to quickly type a response and hit send as it is going through their mind. Emotion has always been there in the past; however, emotion emitted through channels such as text and email may have responses come more

Understand Communication Preferences

quickly and therefore less thoughtfully.

The lack of proofreading and editing during these quick exchanges has caused many communication issues when a message is sent to an unintended recipient (e.g., you are thinking of them when sending), unnecessary multiple recipients (e.g., reply all), and credibility of the sender if there are significant spelling or grammatical errors. In the latter example, the entire meaning of the message can be altered with the omission of a word. For example, "Your request is approved" is a lot different than "Your request is not approved."

You should also understand how your peers and managers would like you to communicate with them, and you should make your expectations known as to how you prefer to communicate. I have had many people who never respond when I send them emails. However, these same individuals are always willing to communicate via instant text message. Some people prefer constant written communication using email and instant text message, and can go back and forth all day. I personally prefer picking up the phone if I see multiple emails and instant messages going back and forth. For example, I have set the example that I prefer not to have an email or instant text message go back and forth more than twice before picking up the phone. However, this is simply my preference. One time, I found I was inadvertently annoying a colleague whenever I sent them an instant message. I would ask if she was available. If she responded "yes" I would provide my phone number to call me. She finally sent me a note asking why I always assumed she was available for a phone call. She was available for the instant text message session, and just didn't know that I preferred the phone.

When possible, we need to understand what works best for everyone and do what we can to accommodate that in the best interest of enhancing the communication experience. The key is to know what works best for the people we communicate with most often. When that isn't clear, ask the obvious but often missed question, "What is the best way to communicate with you?"

38.

Know What the Written Word Says About You

Sometimes I think that the written word is a lost art form. Considering how hard I had to work on improving my own writing skills over the years, I take this topic very seriously. In some cases, the use of proper grammar has disintegrated due to the fast-paced environment and technology all around us. Understanding that language is constantly evolving, I have grown to be flexible and accepting of new styles, forms, and words (look up "Ginormous" to get the point). However, I still understand the importance of how much the written word says about the writer.

Twitter, a social networking platform created in 2006, is a text-based methodology to post your thoughts with less than one hundred and forty characters. These "tweets," for those not familiar, can be made public to anyone who may be following the author. The public nature of this communication channel is a good example of why a writer needs to be extremely careful of what is written—or, in this case, posted. However, the shortened number of characters creates the need for the person posting to use symbols, limit the use of vowels, and eliminate punctuation in many cases. It also opens the reader up to many interpretations of the meaning of the message, the intended emotion, and limited context in which it was written.

Although some employers limit texting, it doesn't eliminate employees from staying in a texting mode when sending written communication through emails, instant messages, and in some cases, official memos. I have often been accused of being critical about professional writing. Texting and instant messaging are so commonplace in today's society, both personally and professionally, that they have influenced grammar when it comes time for formal memos and presentations to be done. Too many times, the habits from these quick-hit communication channels come out when it was not intended.

Know What the Written Word Says About You

I consider attention to detail in writing both common sense and critical to anyone's success in the professional world. I personally enjoy the challenge of creating a perfect document. I try to have a magnetic eye when it comes to spelling errors, spacing errors, and many editorial issues. Although I can hardly say that I am perfect with my own writing, I make the effort. In some cases, I think the diverse communication channels and flow have changed our attention to editing the written word. I don't think we need to push the argument to the full extent and force everyone to hire an editor to sit down and read every email that is sent. However, I would strongly suggest that the authors slow down enough to proofread their own work. Stopping to read what was written prior to sending an email is a smart business move—simply running spell check does not count.

Written communications tell a lot about a person. Are you detail oriented? Do you have a reputation for misspelling, poor grammar, or lack of ability to check your own work? Whether we like it or not, judgments are often being made about our intelligence level based on what we put down in writing. In a professional setting, do you want the reputation of being the person who always uses silly acronyms such as LOL ("Laugh out loud"), EMPHASIZES YOUR EMOTIONS THROUGH CAPITALIZATION, or must get your point across with multiple exclamation points (e.g., !!!!!!!!) on formal, business-related communications? Believe it or not, I have read the word "crap" more than once on supposedly professionally-written emails.

I have been given the advice often that you should assume that what you write or send to someone can, and potentially will, be made public, even if your intentions are to keep the audience restricted. There are far too many opportunities for messages to be sent on to unintended parties. We are too public in our communications in today's world not to be cautious of what we write. I am not talking about spelling issues. I am talking about private messages that become public because of our ability to forward and reply to the message. Emails can become an endless string. I recently saw an example of an email that came back to my inbox over two hundred times because someone hit "Reply All" in error, and then a comedy of emails of people informing the person that she hit "Reply All," followed by the annoyed recipients who chose to inform everyone that they should not be responding to "Reply All." The final kicker was the courtesy "Thanks" response at the end.

I am often surprised—although I have seen it enough not to be—that within minutes following an internal memorandum, it is already published on an external website for the entire world to see. I am not naïve

The Transformation of a Doubting Thomas

enough to think that this is not intentional as a way to get the good news out about a company. However, we need to be sensitive that in any company, less trusted individuals with access to information are hungry to seek out the media to share the negative company news as well.

Depending on the company policy, the written word can be permanent. You should always make the assumption that what you write is considered part of the permanent record. How often have you seen in the news someone from a large corporation been dragged through some investigation, including a senate committee hearing, because of an email that came back to haunt them, or someone running for public office whose past written word forced them to be dragged through the mud? The key is to be careful in what you choose to put down in writing. Deleting your emails may not be your savior with today's technology. We all need to be sensitive in what we choose to send out with our name on it.

Let's oversimplify: proofread your work. The easiest way to do this is to stop and read it before sending it. I know I am stating the obvious, but running spell check is not considered editing in my eyes. Just ask my old manager, who had the word "manger" written at least twenty times throughout one of my performance appraisals. If we don't edit our work, we may be losing some credibility—just ask the person we attempted to recognize with an email that starts with "Congradulations."

I have had many people tell me that writing skills aren't needed for certain jobs, such as being on the phones talking with customers. This may be true based on the job itself, but it also has to do with pride in your own skills and ability. In my field of work starting from speaking to customers on the phone to managing people and projects, I felt it was imperative to have decent writing skills. Let's use the example of working on the phones: You may need to document the conversation on the system. Other customer service representatives need to see it for future interactions. The customer needs it for a record to ensure that the inquiry is addressed and resolved. What if it is more complicated, and an email or written request needs to go to another department? What about emailing the manager for assistance? I have seen run-on sentences that have lost all meaning, and entire communications without a vowel. Basic writing skills are critical if your original intended meaning is to be understood.

The speed of business may have moved us from the need to consciously vet everything written through proper and traditional grammar editing. I am pragmatic and understand not every word needs to be scrutinized. My request of you is to pay attention and double check your own work to ensure clarity within the writing. How it is written, and the attention to detail, is often interpreted solely by the reader, regardless of intent.

Know What the Written Word Says About You

If you are someone who does not proofread well on a computer system, there are other methods that are helpful, such as reading a passage backwards, and in some cases, printing it out to give it the extra attention it may need (note: plug to minimize printing when possible for environmental reasons). You can always have a second set of eyes review as well.

Whether someone chooses texting, instant messaging, email, or formal memos, a person's personality comes out loud and clear. All methods are effective means of communicating. Text and email tend to be more reactive, but knowing this will change how you effectively use it. The key is to think things through before you hit send. These written communication channels have a tendency to have more emotion—which can be dangerous. What you intended to communicate and what is truly interpreted can and will be different. Take the time to gather your thoughts and to review them. Interpretation is a one-sided process. The recipient has full control to interpret your message any way he or she wants. A simple written joke, such as, "What was up with your presentation this morning?" can go from a fun message to say "nice job" with a little jab, to getting the recipient upset and forcing the need for apologies.

When it comes to written communications, please take notice of the following:
- Be clear and concise in what you are attempting to convey
- Invest time to review your written work prior to turning it in or sending it on
- Understand what you write will become a record of who you are
- Writing is a skill that can and should be honed
- There is value in effective writing skills; value that will be noticed and appreciated by the reader.

39.

Learn the Value of Effective Verbal Communication

Learning to verbally communicate effectively is a valuable tool that will build your confidence and credibility. The ability to appropriately balance a message, filter a message, and provide an impactful message is important to move a professional business forward. An effective communication style and approach will give the presenter confidence, and gain credibility with the audience.

What is "effective" communication? The term itself is vague, and therefore hard to define. I like to start with the basics. What is the message you want to send? Whether you are attempting to put two sentences together or a thirty-minute presentation, you must have a clear message with a strong beginning and a strong conclusion. The message you are attempting to convey should be emphasized and reiterated throughout the body of your presentation. The preparation in formulating your message is important, even in question and answer formats or impromptu situations. You should know your audience well enough to have some semblance of an idea of the types of questions or responses that may come up. For example, an executive summary doesn't need the minute details of the inner workings of a process. This type of audience simply wants to be assured that the process will work as intended. You can give high-level examples where this is the case and have details available if questions are asked, or in the Appendix at the back of the written presentation.

Even if you have the jitters when communicating in front of a group, keep them under control and attempt to present confidently. I realize this is easy to say and harder to do. As you nurture your ability to control your nerves, that ability will improve over time. Keep trying, even if mistakes are made. The more public speaking you do, the more comfortable you will be. I have seen too many people in meeting settings who were experts in their fields not say anything because they were uncomfortable with

Learn the Value of Effective Verbal Communication

their own oral communication skills. Not saying a word is communication—if you choose not to participate, you must take this into consideration. If a question is asked about any additional points or a discussion is required prior to a vote, for example, you can make a difference in the direction a business takes if you choose to stay out of the debate. Be confident enough to state your points. You do not have to own the situation; you need to just confidently speak up when necessary. Confidence comes with time and practice.

How often have you been distracted when a presenter communicates a message intertwined with filler words, such as "ah," "um," and "you know?" There are plenty of filler words out there. Many times, the speaker's mind is working faster than he can get the words out as he thinks ahead to the next piece of the presentation. This is easier to fix than you think. Being conscious of your own behavior is half the battle. When you begin to understand how distracting or annoying it can be to the audience, you will slow down your thought process and formulate better-constructed sentences. You can have people around you provide feedback. This practice is critical in a Toastmasters meeting and has been a practical exercise to everyone who has ever had anyone count their filler words.

The ability to reduce filler words will increase your credibility with others. Although you may feel embarrassed at first, the respect you will gain from your audience for your improved communication will easily make up for it. You may remember the story of Caroline Kennedy when she expressed an interest in the U.S. Senate seat in New York. In a thirty-minute interview in December 2008, she had been reported to say "you know" well over one hundred times. The unpopular media responses hurt her credibility. It was not long after the media stories that she decided to drop out of the race. If it was not the direct link to her dropping out, was it at least a contributing factor?

The best written speech is only as good as the person presenting it. Imagine the "Gettysburg Address" wrought with filler words: "Four score, ah, and um seven years ago, you know, our fathers brought forth, you know, upon this ah continent, um a new nation, you know conceived in um liberty, and, um, dedicated to the, you know, proposition that all men are created equal." You get the point.

While I am discussing effective communication, I thought I would also share some of my favorite communication pet peeves. I'll start with the use of the words "go" or "went" when the intended word was "say" or "said." For example, "He went, 'You should have…'" Another one is "to be honest with you." It adds no value to the conversation, and does not change the message. The phrase may even negatively impact your

The Transformation of a Doubting Thomas

credibility since it provides the audience with a taste of something about to be said that needed emphasis on the so-called truth. The phrase is filler and should be avoided. I went years saying the word "supposebly." Ask me to spell it out on paper and I would spell it correctly, "supposedly." I knew how to say it, but picked up on the habit of saying it like I had been hearing it from several people around me. Someone said to me once, "You realize the word is <u>supposedly</u>?" Yes, I did, but I had become oblivious to my own poor habits. Actively listen for it. It is still out there in the professional world being used daily.

Another unnecessary phrase is, "It is what it is." What is "it"? What new nugget of hope or information is the audience given with the phrase? I find it is a way to end a conversation, but adds very little value to the intended message. Remember, your conclusion is just as important as the introduction and body of your message. Do you really want to end a presentation or a conversation with, "It is what it is"? Finally, the recent integration of the words "right" and "really" at the end of sentences is becoming main stream. For example, "You know what I'm saying, right?" Or a little increase in tone when someone ends with a sarcastic, "So that's what happened? Really?" A keen ear, or in many cases, a not- so-keen ear, can easily pick up on these add-on words that add little to no value to the conversation.

Build your own confidence and credibility by starting with the basics. Keep the message clear and concise, and speak with confidence. Minimize filler words and nurture your ability to overcome your butterflies and your audience will gain respect and consequently promote your credibility. Your verbal communication will become a valuable tool with direct links to your success.

40.

Take Action – Hope Won't Win the Game without a Game Plan

Whether you are moving your business forward or moving yourself forward, you can't hope for the best and expect it every time. You need to take action and put in the right game plan and preparation to ensure that your hope is given the appropriate direction and momentum. I have heard people who were responsible for multi-million dollar businesses say that they hope the new idea or initiative works. I truly believe in some cases that their fingers were crossed. We can't predict the outcome of every decision or action we take; however, we can dictate the direction and significantly increase our odds by taking out the unknowns.

I was meeting with one of the people I mentor. It was our second meeting, so we were following up on actions I had asked of her in our last meeting. I asked her to come back with three names of leaders she wanted to emulate and network with. We spent almost an hour discussing the benefits of networking, and how we could work together to gain confidence to pave her own road ahead. During our discussion we talked about networking with people a couple of levels ahead of her. I was excited to see who she had come up with, whether it was someone from across the country or a completely different line of business. She brought in two names of people within one hundred yards of her and a name of a member of her own management team. Although it was not what I had expected, it was the small circle of names she knew.

I realized then that her circle of influence was small, and her networking circle was not much bigger. I also realized that she was accustomed to not taking accountability unless it was specifically asked of her and then followed up with a formal request. We discussed the benefits of taking action immediately and taking responsibility for requests independently. Taking action would contribute to her confidence and success.

Our continued conversation made it clear that she had issues

The Transformation of a Doubting Thomas

understanding our corporation as a whole. I shared numerous examples of my own inability to understand our particular corporate culture early on and what had been required to be more proactive. I was able to share live examples of when this had worked. She still seemed hesitant. I almost felt as though she "hoped" I would do some of this for her in our mentoring sessions.

I had to change her hopeful mentality to one of action. So, I began to give examples of instances when we hear a request and are not sure whether we should do something about it or not. We discussed the benefits of clarifying and confirming the requests to ensure that the appropriate owner and action comes out of the meeting or interaction. How many times have you run into an old friend and said, "We should get together some time," and nothing ever comes to fruition? This is the same concept. Action is required for successful execution of a request. Action makes it happen, not hope.

I found one of the potential people she wanted to network with could be seen simply by standing up and looking into the office. The fact that she identified someone to network with—even locally—was a small stretch for her, but a good first step. Another person she identified was two levels up from her, but within the same line of business. She said she had met with him when he was in town a few months before. I was excited that she had growing confidence enough to answer these questions and seek to expand her circle of influence. This was another small win, since I had not expected her to have had any previous contact with him yet. Although the networking meeting was more a circumstance of the situation, she took advantage of the opportunity. She was starting to put the pieces together regarding how advantageous this would be for her growth potential.

Her meeting with the person on the management team put her slightly out of her comfort zone, which was a plus, as it demonstrated to her that she had survived and was building her confidence one step at a time. She mentioned that this individual had said they should get together every couple of months to share ideas and discuss her progress. I was ecstatic and asked when the meeting had taken place. She said that it was about three weeks prior to the meeting we were having. I asked what was holding her back from following up to organize the next meeting with him. She said she did not know; maybe she hoped they could catch up in a couple months. Hope would not move her forward. I know, because I sat back and waited for people to approach me far too many times myself.

People hold back on taking action for many reasons. Sometimes, we

Take Action—Hope Won't Win the Game without a Game Plan

just forget. This can be easily resolved if we write it down or set it up immediately. For others, it is pushing beyond their comfort level. Confidence comes with time, after continuing to do something over and over again. I often hear, "I don't want to bother (insert name here)." If you never ask, you will never know the answer. Finally, there may be a lack of understanding as to the expectations within a corporate culture. Ask questions. Curiosity is only going to broaden your cultural understanding and comfort.

Our mentor conversation continued to what she wanted to gain from the three individuals she'd selected. She mentioned that she had watched the other two people already in close proximity to her over the past month. I asked what she had gained from watching them. It was a difficult question for her, since she hadn't been sure what she had been looking for. The question was not intended to put her on the spot. The question's intention was to let her know that she had gleaned a month's worth of valuable observations. Now, what was she going to do about it? She began to grasp the concept that she needed to take action by either trying some of the things she'd seen herself, or by meeting with these two leaders to get some context to what she'd seen so that she could begin to apply it. In simple terms, her personal growth would accelerate when she took action.

We moved on to the next long-term steps she wanted to take. She stated that she wanted to take the next step up in her area or move to another area. She understood the direction of our conversation and proactively mentioned that she did not have a game plan. She was going to wait until something opened up and she would put in her application and résumé. When I asked if we could review her résumé, she said she hadn't written one yet. I asked how she planned on submitting it if the opening came up today? She said she would have to scramble. This was another "aha" moment for her, and it was fun for me to watch this learning take place before my eyes. We discussed how I "hoped" someone would have had this conversation with me years before. She immediately began to take her own actions right there in the meeting. She began to outline the beginning of her résumé, she took copious notes, and I know that her future success was now in motion based on her actions.

We must all have a game plan, whether it is for our own career, or to push an initiative over the finish line. If you don't have a game plan, sit with someone who can help formulate one with you. Finding help and support is taking action.

41.

Learn to Manage Up, Down, and Around

Can you manage and motivate people around you effectively? Can you inspire the people who work for you and with you to run through a wall for you? Can you push your peers forward who only come in for their paycheck? Can you confidently influence leaders above you and make a difference? I have found that professionals are not always equally balanced in all of the above. This presents an opportunity to learn to better manage up, down, and around. The number of people who work for us, with us, or above us is irrelevant. Everyone has a boss, even CEOs and self-employed people, both of whom need to report back to shareholders and customers, respectively. Everyone has people all around that can be influenced, persuaded, motivated, and managed.

Let's start with the people who work for you. Many of us have been in positions in which we need to manage down. However, I should rephrase it to describe it as lead down. We should be leading people along a path to success. In this day and age, people want and need to feel appreciated and feel as though they are a part of the overall company. Managing has to be replaced with leading if we truly want to have the impact necessary to drive the business forward and build an effective relationship with employees.

Today's workforce thirsts for leaders who can build confidence, develop relationships, and increase people's overall satisfaction level. The success of the business is only as good as those who are doing the work. So I will ask the question that was posed to me, "If you ran through a wall, would people follow?" It took me many more years to learn that you can, and will, get better results by caring for people. I found out that I needed to be more open to what they have to say to improve the business, and strive to make them better today than they were yesterday. I needed to adapt my style based on the individual I was dealing with, rather than blanket managing a group. I learned I needed to lead the effort, not just manage the day-to-day results. I also realized that if I peaked over my shoulder as I ran through the wall, I wasn't exactly sure if I would see people following me. I had to work harder and smarter at knowing the answer. Since I am confident that hope won't win the game, I began to put in the effort needed to ensure that I wouldn't have to look over my shoulder any longer. In many cases, I was learning to not only run through the wall, but to get out of the way so my team could forge ahead. I was learning to ride the coat-tails of others while leading.

I was gaining confidence in the fact that people believed in my vision, my mission, and my core values. I became more accepting of employees as individuals, and became more myself. I used to worry that if I ever played the trust game, in which you fall back into someone else's arms, that I would not be caught. I truly believe that when I began to genuinely trust and respect the efforts of the people around me, those people became more satisfied and productive. I became less obsessed with results and more focused on the individuals working toward those results. Having less control was a new and uncomfortable concept to me. To my amazement, however, the results did indeed take care of themselves.

Another lesson is to take care of the support people, whether they work directly for you or not. The people who do the little things (and the big things) behind the scenes keep a business afloat. The many little things add up to significant impacts to everyone's workload, potential profit, and overall satisfaction levels. I have been in several positions when people on the support staff have been on vacation and I immediately felt the short-term impacts. I have also been witness to instances when people on the support staff have been let go from the company due to budget cuts. I have felt the pain of picking up the workload nobody realized was there until it was too late. There were impacts to communication channels, key contacts, and routines that vanished. I was so confident in certain things getting done like clockwork that many things came to a screeching halt when the support person left.

I understand business models revolving around expense management, but we need to fully consider the value of good support and build that into the overall model. Everyone in the company doesn't need a dedicated staff working behind the scenes, but a good business model does account for the value added by having a solid support staff. The 'go-to folks' are go to for a reason. They will take care of you. When you have the advantage of great support people, always ask what you can do for them. It is a question that I may not ask enough, but I do know it is always appreciated.

Managing peers around you is difficult for many reasons. How do you

The Transformation of a Doubting Thomas

manage people or situations when you supposedly have very little influence on them? They do not have to listen to someone who is not an authority figure for them. I have learned to build bridges, and I am very confident that I have a positive reputation for working well with my peers.

As I have stated many times, it was not always that way. I had a demanding and urgent nature to my requests. To some extent, I don't think the urgency has ever left me. However, I now better understand the importance of collaboration. In recent years, I've had fewer people reporting directly to me, but seemed to have more responsibility across a broader spectrum. I had no choice in these situations but to learn to manage the peers with whom I had no direct influence. I had to invest the time to speak to people who could assist and support me. I had to work well with people who could teach me a new business, or learn to negotiate their involvement in order to assist with the completion of one of my requests. I learned how to provide mutually conducive environments in which everyone could win. I also taught myself that it was all right to not have all the answers and to ask questions…A lot of questions. I learned not to hold back and to ask questions that allowed people to dig deeper, and this in turn, built mutual trust and respect. I learned that a team of peers who learned from each other and played off of everyone's strengths all moved up together.

I also learned to eliminate my negative competitive feelings. I used to worry whether the person with whom I was working would get the credit for work I had done. Would they get the next promotion? Could I afford to have them look better than me? When I finally learned that a team effort creates better quality work, we both won. I began to get a reputation for being a team player and that made me more favorable in the eyes of people making decisions about my next roles. I am not naïve enough to think that there is no competition. However, I no longer worry about it. I trust that either the right person will get the job or, more importantly, that everyone wins in the right situation.

How do you manage the people above you? This is a foreign concept to many people. I have learned that we need to learn to communicate up effectively. If you are given feedback, you have the right to ask for examples. If you are told to do something faster or better, you must ask how and why. A healthy and respectful dialogue will build the relationship and make both of you stronger. If you do not understand specific instructions, you should clarify and confirm. It may bother some managers to have to go into more details, but it is much better to invest the time up front than waste energy doing it all over again due to some initial miscommunication resulting in the job being done wrong. The confidence you possess when speaking to people you manage should not go away just because the bigwig is in the room. Nothing should change. We are all working toward the same company goal of making our business better.

We should seek to maintain strong conviction in our voice and avoid holding back points we feel need to be said. If we prepare and use facts to state our points, we should be confident in what we are discussing, as this discussion may create opinions and create a debate that is needed. If you are not strong enough to state your opinion, then all sides of the argument are not exhibited and additional facts are left off to the side. If your leader disagrees with your points, this is fine since at least then the entire story is on the table. When this occurs, you should professionally ask questions as to why the leader may not agree with you if you feel you have stated all the appropriate facts. Finish your thoughts with confidence. Even if cut off, you can professionally interject when you feel it is appropriate, or ask to finish your thoughts. I am not asking for everyone to speak over their managers, but I have found if you have done the legwork and preparation, including building a solid relationship foundation, this type of communication is acceptable, and even encouraged, as everyone is striving to achieve the company goals.

I have found people who were more willing to offer a quick apology for having an opinion than willing to finish a healthy debate. I was one of those people. Now, I seek to ensure that it is a two-way conversation. This comes through mutual engagement in the conversation and a built-up trust and respect from both parties. If this mutual trust and respect is not there, then make the effort to build it. Be open and honest; the buzz word in professional lingo is to be transparent. Do not be deceitful or withhold information. Note that I didn't say you couldn't filter messages; filtering messages provides enough information without wasting anyone's time (e.g., executive summary).

Be as prepared as possible to manage up by having reference information at your fingertips, staying in tune with industry information, and understanding the leader's tendencies. Keep a nice pace to what you are saying so it is fully understood and questions can be asked. Be structured and organized with your thoughts; take the time to think it through. Trust that when you are in a position to speak to senior people within the organization, you are there to provide valuable information and that they are there to seek information that will strengthen the business.

I have had many conversations with individuals who felt there was an underlying tone or agenda to some of the senior leader questions asked in focus-group-type sessions. For example, cynics may perk up when responding to a question like, "How do you think we are doing overall

The Transformation of a Doubting Thomas

as a company?" when they are having issues with their own management team, and feel the question is meant to spark a negative comment. If that is truly the case, escalate your concerns to other parties who could make a difference. Trust is a delicate thing that needs to be earned, but it is a two-way street. You have the right to build up enough trust so that when someone asks what's on your mind, you can genuinely share it.

The other side is not to speak up just to be heard or to impress. You should speak up when you have something important to say, not because you have a scripted or canned question or response.

Get comfortable with having conversations with senior leaders. Be curious—ask questions that are meaningful to you and your team. Your silence says as much as the person asking questions just to be heard—yes, that is obvious too. It takes work and preparation to increase your comfort level. You can role play ahead of time and network with people outside your area to practice. In all cases, seek to build your confidence by continuing to try. You may surprise yourself.

Whether you are managing up, down, or around, know the audience and balance your messages with honest and genuine responses. There is no need for the traditional good-bad-good sandwich feedback approach. Just provide honest answers and questions. Look for the positive in everything, but build relationships in which direct and genuine conversations can take place—that is where constructive conversations grow. If something is not going right, it is not about spin, it is about what positive measures you are taking to fix it. If two people can work through a plan of action, anything can be made better.

Finally, be willing to be wrong. Take chances—it won't hurt you (most of the time) as long as the right effort and attitude are there. The great thing about all of the mistakes I've made is that I get the excitement of sharing what I've learned with everyone willing to listen. This builds your credibility and trust—thus opening up communication with more people. If I didn't make mistakes, I would have no speeches or books to write, or have anything to say to my mentors.

42.

Laugh at Work; Laugh With Others

I used to provide newer people at work a business overview once a month. I would go into the classroom and spend about an hour talking about my business. I tried to be as engaging as possible and attempted to add some interesting stories and humor to the presentation. We would get evaluations back, and every once and a while I would get one back that said I was funny. My wife has often said, "You're just not funny, but that's not what I love about you," then we both laugh at ourselves. I have a tendency to get straight to the point and straight to work in the professional environment. She said enough with that comment to remind me to enjoy myself at work and to inject humor, on occasion, to get through tough times, or to just enjoy a laugh with colleagues for the sake of a laugh.

Earlier in my professional career, I had a serious undertone to my working style. I was too uptight and often too businesslike when a good laugh would have been better. I was inconsistently funny in some situations, and attempted to be funny in other times when it was not appropriate. I knew when a laugh was needed, but attempted too hard to make it happen.

I have found, early on, through Toastmasters, and by observing fellow colleagues who could effectively work a meeting with well-timed humor, that it is a communication tool. If I worked hard enough on my speeches and presentations, and consciously applied humor, I could have a more positive influence on the people around me since they remained engaged. I may never be considered a comedian, but I was starting to pick up that humorous communication is a learned trait and must be honed. Humorous communication is about timing and delivery, and about how to effectively use the tool. I still had work to do on my humorous side, but I saw the value.

Humor can be an effective form of communication. If the person

The Transformation of a Doubting Thomas

attempting humor is not considered funny, it can be an ineffective form of communication. I will state the obvious and note that humor can be inappropriate, poorly timed, or offensive—be aware of the audience, timing, and potential impacts.

There were times when I knew I was trying too hard in my attempts to slip in a funny comment that wasn't natural for me. In many cases, it may have been blurted out of nervousness. One of my managers hit me between the eyes with feedback once by telling me to relax. I knew my body language at the time showed tension. The manager followed up the comment, "You need to relax," with, "and you can be really boring, at times." Ouch. It's tough when someone is so dead-on accurate with his or her feedback. We discussed it further. He was making the point that we had laughed together in the past and he enjoyed that side of me. He wanted me to be more myself. We also discussed timing and style. I know that I am not a natural story or joke teller. But, I do enjoy self-deprecating humor and appropriately timed one-liners in my personal time; I just had difficulty carrying that over to the professional side. If I learned to be a better storyteller, I could transform my style to one that would possibly reduce my own anxiety, improve my satisfaction level, and change the perception of people around me.

Do you remember that my wife said I'm not funny? In reality, my wife and my manager were both right. I needed to be more of myself at work and enjoy the ride. Toastmasters International has annual humorous contests. I heard tenured members say that the humorous speech was the hardest speech to write. However, they also emphasized that it is an important part of communication. If you can react effectively to a joke, or actively tell a story that can keep an audience's interest and make them laugh, you are winning in the game of communication. I had to work hard at acting naturally to create memorable speeches that grabbed the audience's attention through humor. I gained more audience reaction and increased my confidence level the more I did it. As I "practiced" being more myself and being less prescribed with what I said and how and when I said it, I was able to be more personable in my interactions. I was turning into someone I already was—the person I was outside of work. I was starting to be perceived as less uptight and even funny, at times.

The goal was not to be a comedian, but to be able to relax and be an active part of any engaging conversation. I became more conscious of my own enjoyment at work. I could also see how people seemed to be enjoying our conversations more. I now periodically get a note that says, "Thanks for making me laugh today…I needed it." I have heard that more often over the last few years from people who worked with me in the past. They have gone out of their way to mention how they enjoyed this side of me and had no idea I had this type of personality. These comments go a long way in increasing my confidence level.

I ended up finishing third in my first Toastmasters Humorous Speech Contest for our Division in 2009. The division represented the state of Maine and a small part of New Hampshire. I was proud of myself. I entered a contest for humor when I knew I had to work very hard at being funny. I was learning through Toastmasters, and through better self awareness and practice about my "looser" communication style, I was learning to find my true voice. I even won the division humorous contest in 2011. I was breaking out of my serious shell and having good laughs with others along the way. I now try to consistently incorporate natural humor into my presentations and speeches to get across key points, and in some cases, purely for entertainment purposes. My satisfaction with work has been through the roof over the past several years. So has my productivity and quality of work; and so has my success. It is not a coincidence.

43.

Build and Maintain a Strong Résumé

If you are looking for a job, résumés can be the difference between getting your foot in the door and getting a rejection letter without being granted an interview. Résumés are, at times, our first and only impression on a prospective company or new position. The importance of an effective résumé is typically not lost on those seeking a job. However, what about people who already have a job? Unless you work in a small company where you know everyone, a résumé works the same way by allowing others to get to know you professionally.

You should always have an updated résumé ready. The practice of building and maintaining a strong résumé is not always related to active job searching. The routine of keeping an updated résumé is to eliminate surprise pressures when something of interest does come up or someone wants to get to know you professionally. A prepared résumé that can be instantly obtained shows your preparation when someone may ask for it. This has happened to me more than once. It also ensures that you stay up to date and not forget about including key accomplishments. If a question comes up relating to recent accomplishments, you are ready to share instantly and are in a position for effective networking conversations. I have seen far too many people scrambling to put together a résumé because they were caught off guard.

Résumé writing is a skill that can be taught. When preparing a résumé, the key is due diligence and constant review. A résumé should always be considered a work in progress. There is no better tool in your arsenal than a résumé as a way to express yourself professionally in writing. With that said, I have seen résumés that were slapped together quickly with very little thought. I have also seen people pay a lot of money for someone else to put together a résumé that ultimately looked like it was put together just as quickly. If you are going to pay someone, be an active part of the process. No one knows you better than yourself. If you invest the time and get the right support, you will be proud of the work of art you put together.

A résumé is potentially a one-time shot to make that great first impression. You can't afford to submit a document with spelling errors, with glaring grammatical errors, or a poor overall layout. The amount of time invested in a résumé is obvious. Often, readers are turned off because of the lack of visual stimulation and obvious errors as they glance over the information. This can occur before they even begin to read the content in detail. How a résumé presents itself on the page tells a very big story about you. Effectively organized résumés should point the eyes of the reader to the right places to help with the flow and readability. The appropriate investment ensures that it is the best-quality story possible.

When is the last time you touched your résumé? I review mine quarterly and I am not shopping for a job. I have a recurring appointment that pops up on my online calendar. After the initial investment to put the full document together, I invest about five minutes per quarter into maintaining it. I learned early in my professional life not to have a dusty résumé. Growing up with a father with over twenty-five years of Human Resources experience with Sears Roebuck & Co., and my subsequent twenty years of interviewing job candidates taught me to always be prepared.

My analysis on retaining employees, my recruiting experience, and interviewing has allowed me to see hundreds, if not thousands, of résumés. The following are tips to help you to build and maintain a strong résumé.

- **Style.** There is no right or wrong style. The Internet has plenty of websites dedicated to résumé styles and formats. I have yet to find two that are exactly alike, which should clearly tell you there is no magic formula. However, while there is no right or wrong, there is still a first impression.
- **Bullets versus sentences.** I personally think it is a preference and that it doesn't matter as long you are consistent, clear, concise, and succinct with your information.
- **Use of effective spacing and layout.** Proper spacing and open areas on the document grab attention. Don't crowd the document with words. Use the open areas to your advantage to ensure that key items catch the attention of the readers and point their eyes to the key words/places on the document.
- **Hesitancy in sharing.** Go out there and share it with everyone. There are a couple of reasons for this. First, you need a third party's opinion and proofreading skills. Another set of eyes is a must. I had someone

The Transformation of a Doubting Thomas

review my résumé recently and she found an extra space that had been there for years. Second, share your résumé for networking purposes. Having your résumé floating around is not a bad thing when it gets into the right hands. You will also surprise some readers who may not know all of your background. The only assumption you should make with a résumé is that no one knows you.

- **Editing.** Running spell check doesn't count as editing. Enough said.
- **Routines.** Have a recurring calendar appointment to update your résumé quarterly. No need to think about it, just do it.
- **Jargon.** Match your résumé language and headings consistent to job descriptions, but avoid internal jargon. You can use language familiar to people in your company if you are using your résumé internally, or use similar language to a job advertisement you are applying for. For example, if you have a sales background and you are pursuing a marketing position, use terms such as "Marketed products to…" However, when possible, I try to minimize the amount of changes by staying broad enough with your terminology that both internal and external readers can understand it, so you only need to maintain one document. In large companies, you also can't assume people in different departments are familiar with all internal terminology.
- **Be specific.** Assume the people you may be speaking to do not understand your past jobs or responsibilities. Be specific. Even if you are meeting with someone who is familiar with the job description, use specifics on your résumé that differentiate you individually.
- **Use statistics.** Job descriptions should include powerful information that shows the size and scale of your responsibilities; numbers can be insightful (e.g., Collected on 5-million dollar portfolio, exceeded goal by over twenty-five percent for twelve consecutive months). Dollars and percentages visually stand out.
- **Word choice.** Avoid support language (e.g., Assisted…) and use language that shows your leadership (e.g., Created, Directed, Prepared, Piloted, and Developed).
- **What makes you special?** Use differentiating accomplishments and descriptions. What makes you unique? Go beyond the duties and tasks of the job.
- **Order of facts.** Key points should be prioritized in the job descriptions. For example, "Managed as many as fifty people" should be placed ahead of "Maintained timesheets" in your job assessment.
- **Final document.** There is no such thing. Your résumé is a fluid document. You need to adapt it regularly and as needed.
- **Outside experiences.** Include assets and experiences that may not

have a direct link to the job in which you are interested, but show differentiating and special features. A friend of mine had a résumé that didn't list his Military reserves experience. Not including these details instantly neglected over fifteen years of critical leadership, commitment, and service to our country.

- **Volunteer work.** Don't forget to include your volunteer activities and other skills, regardless of what you are interested in. Volunteering shows you can balance time and responsibilities and shows you give back to the community.
- **Certifications.** You should include appropriate certifications and system proficiency. For example, you can write "Proficient in Microsoft PowerPoint and Microsoft Excel" if it's applicable to your knowledge and background. Also include key certifications, such as "Six Sigma Green Belt Certified."
- **How personal?** Include personal items if they strengthen your cause. For example, you may add something like, "Perfect attendance five consecutive years," and "Excellent health—run twenty miles per week." Both examples differentiate you from a typical résumé and show that you will come to work energized and ready every day. Another example might read, "Married for fifteen years." Although employers can't discriminate or even ask questions based on your marital status or health, it proactively rounds out your full story and shows more personal differentiation and stability.
- **Sequence of events.** The most common formats are chronological and skills-based (e.g., jobs, volunteer work, and training). Just like résumé styles, this can come down to personal preference, unless you have done your homework and found that your company of interest has their own preferences.

If you don't have a résumé, or have not touched your résumé in the last three months, pull it out and start today. You never know when you will need it. Make it a work of art.

44.

Manage Your Time, Don't Let it Manage You – Part I

I have found in my over twenty years of professional experience that poor time management skills are one of the biggest pitfalls for leaders. I am going to intentionally repeat myself: poor time management skills are one of the biggest pitfalls for leaders. I took organization training over eighteen years ago, and I understood at that time the power of managing my day and beyond. More importantly, I realized I couldn't survive in the business world until I could manage the swirling days, weeks, and months around me. By actively staying organized, I found I could dedicate the appropriate time to urgent and important items, spend more time developing people, and yes, put out those dreadful fires that often come our way.

When you are running at capacity, the fire drill exercise will sacrifice something else that may need to be dropped. However, if you have full control and knowledge of your own capacity, you can not only do it right, but you have a chance to do it all, and more. Included in this section are highlights from an evolving organization course I have taught over the years for new and experienced managers. I have a positive reputation for being highly organized at work. Some call it being anal retentive or compulsive. However, very few people can remember me ever missing a key deadline.

First and foremost, people are the highest priority. Regardless of your job responsibilities or what is on your calendar for the day, people who work for you take the top billing. As a manager, how do you get all of the administrative work done if you are constantly bombarded with questions from your direct reports? Good managers can anticipate questions and concerns through staff meetings and team meetings. It is extremely important to lay out clear expectations and preparations, including what might be the best time to connect with you, what is on your plate for the

Manage Your Time, Don't Let it Manage You—Part I

day, and who to contact if you are not available. Being ahead of the game is also important. You can do this by anticipating common questions and put answers in your reports' hands before the questions are even asked. Everyone wins.

Managers should also understand the most effective ways to present information to a particular audience. Knowing who you are presenting to and how well they will absorb the information is critical. How does your group like to be taught? For example, a manager might find success in asking open-ended questions to ensure clarity. Tossing facts and figures at a group of people and expecting them to remember can be difficult. There should be interaction and engagement from everyone. The group of people learning should feel comfortable, and the leader should invest the appropriate amount of time when it is all over. Sometimes in the past, I rushed information to people by talking at them, and was always surprised when I got a question later about the same subject. I have found it extremely helpful for time-management purposes to invest the time up front so that everyone learns and digests the information from the start. Group settings are extremely helpful in avoiding duplicate messages. If you are not a leader, you should ensure that this gets practiced by discussing this with your manager.

Leaders need to build time into their calendars for the unexpected. How can you do this if you don't know what's coming relating to those "I need it now" requests? If you are scheduled for an eight hour day, and your calendar is booked for that entire eight hours, it is guaranteed that you will not get everything done. The unexpected will happen during that time—I promise. I like to block off time in my day with follow-up items that occupy space on my calendar to cover loose ends. The blocks of time also allow flexibility if meetings go over or someone needs me for something important. These blocks of time are great for reflecting on past meetings, preparing for upcoming meetings, or conducting in-depth work.

You should also schedule time to get away from your desk. This builds in another block of time for the unexpected, and allows extra time for the flexibility to take a break and stay fresh. Below are some additional tips for the unexpected:

• **Schedule time for emails, return messages, etc.** This minimizes your need to multitask and builds more open time. If you build an hour a day for this and it only takes thirty minutes, take advantage of the bonus time for other tasks.

• **Build in time for daily operations and be sensitive to potential impacts within your business.** For example, in a call center, Mondays

The Transformation of a Doubting Thomas

are often high call volume days. Managers are needed on the floor. Build that time on the floor into your calendar for non-meeting activities. Do not schedule your staff meetings during peak times, since the chances for interruption are high and a less productive meeting will occur.

- **Use miscellaneous blocks of time on your calendar for routine events that may not require a specific time.** For example, you know you need two hours tomorrow to provide feedback to people on your team, or do a daily task like quality monitoring. You may schedule it for 10:00 A.M.-12:00 noon. The actual time is not as important as reserving the block of time of two hours. You can build in the flexibility to move this block of time through the same day as you need to as long as you remain committed to making it happen. Be careful of pushing it too late into the day, when you risk not completing it and are required to move it to another day. When you start carrying appointments over to other days, you run the risk of creating a bottleneck situation. For example, pushing the two hours to another day puts you four hours in the hole the following day.
- **Use recurring meetings to hold future times and dates.** This habit gives people a heads up to reserve times and dates and should increase attendance to key meetings. It is respectful of other people's calendars, since it will give everyone ample time to know what is ahead for them, and they can look forward to the same time and date each week or month.

One of the greatest things I did for my own sanity was to keep a pad of paper near my nightstand at home. How does this relate to time management? When random thoughts pop into my head at night, I write them down immediately. The benefits are as follows: 1) I don't forget, thus I don't waste time trying to remember, 2) I sleep better knowing I have immediately addressed my thoughts, 3) I have stronger ideas since I have reached the inner non-stressed part of my brain and can formulate a plan of action. All of this allows me to enter into my day knowing where and when things are happening, with a clear plan of attack to get it done.

Don't be a slave to your calendar, but be committed to it and avoid constant appointment pushing. Consistent appointment pushing to another day is a red flag that you need to change the calendar process—it is either too full or you need to be more committed to it.

You should invest ample time in understanding your future calendar appointments. Organize tomorrow before leaving today. You should invest five minutes before leaving for the day. I make very few promises, but I will make an exception. I promise you will sleep better knowing exactly what's on your plate tomorrow. You should actually schedule

Manage Your Time, Don't Let it Manage You—Part I

this five minute event for the end of day as a calendar appointment. Five invested minutes will save you hours later. Additionally, organize the next week every Friday. Look out a week at a time. Again, schedule this Friday event on your calendar. Finally, organize each month with a few days before the current month ends. Look out a month at a time. Once again, schedule this event on your calendar. This shouldn't be done on the thirtieth of the month—it should be done around the twenty-sixth to avoid surprises in the first week of the following month. The outlook a month ahead of time allows you to determine what normal routines you need to conduct each month and how to spread them accordingly. When we have certain obligations that are required on a monthly basis, I find as high as ninety-five percent of the people on any given month, if given the choice, will do the task at the end of the month. Be in the minority and get things done before they are scheduled and due.

We are in a culture of procrastinators. I am on the opposite end of the spectrum, almost to the extreme, viewing it as the antithesis of procrastination. I want tasks out of the way as quickly as possible so that I can concentrate on other things. I front load certain events in the first or second week of each month to get them out of the way, and allow flexibility in case other events come up that need to be accomplished prior to the month ending. There have been many times when something did come up at the end of the month, and a number of leaders did not meet their requirements as a result. Keeping ahead of your schedule allows for the unexpected. As I was going through my career growing pains, it was effective time management that often kept me afloat.

45.

Manage Your Time, Don't Let it Manage You — Part II

Be realistic with your time frames. Don't be a 'go-getter' that finds many commitments unfulfilled. You don't want to sign up for five projects and not do them on time or on budget. You want to be seen as being on top of your game rather than someone who does a bunch of things averagely or not at all. There are times when you need to build in the extra time for testing, for fine tuning, and building in time for the unexpected. This is called "Under-promising and over-delivering."

You want to be realistic with expectations. You don't want a reputation of "sandbagging" everything so you always look like a hero. You can't say that your team is struggling and will only reach eighty-five percent of the quota, when you know the group will achieve one-hundred percent. This practice does become obvious after a while. The point here is to be pragmatic with your forecasting and communication. Don't tell the requester it will be done by five o'clock P.M. because you 'hope' it will be done by five o'clock P.M. Tell the requester because it *will* be done by that time. If you get it done early, call it a bonus. If the five o'clock deadline isn't the right expectation, be honest and tell the requester when the right time is for it to get done. Please note that there will be deadlines that are non-negotiable requests. The non-negotiable deadlines will impact your other work. If you have practiced preparation for this scenario, you will be able to effectively balance your other commitments, adjust time frames, and be realistic with your communication of expectations. If adjustments negatively influence this request or others, it is always important to keep open lines of communication with the requestor.

Have you thought of everything? In any so-called normal day, have you accounted for everything you need to do in that day? This might include travel time, office visits, walking the floor, and casual conversations with fellow associates. Although you may not 'schedule' these

Manage Your Time, Don't Let it Manage You—Part II

events, they do take your time. Have you accounted for this time and understood the impact it will have? How many times have you been a few minutes late because of a hallway discussion?

I have consistently heard in focus groups and years of management that one of the biggest employee frustration points is a lack of follow through. Respect for you—regardless of your role as a manager, peer, and colleague—can quickly be lost if you don't do what you said would be done. This impacts customers, peers, and subordinates alike. Follow-up is one of the most important things you can do as a leader. The follow-up items may pile one on top of another and become countless. I personally can't remember a lot of things at once. You should make follow-up a mindless exercise. I let my calendar do it all for me and I simply need to wait for the automatic reminder to tell me what to do. If I have done the Day Before, Week Before, Month Before time-management exercise, I won't be surprised. You can be proactive by using your calendar for follow-up appointments, such as return calls, customer callbacks, or employee requests. If you have requested someone else to complete a task by a certain date, you can also make that a follow-up appointment to check in.

Additionally, you should schedule deadlines and preparation for appointments before they are due. If you owe a deliverable for five o'clock P.M. Thursday, the appointment should not be seen for the first time at five o'clock the day it is due. Build the appointment into your calendar when it makes the most sense for you, as long as you have plenty of time for a second look, revisions (there are always revisions), and time for the unexpected. You can use pop-up reminders to your advantage to not only meet deadlines, but to beat deadlines.

Time management is often misunderstood. It takes diligence and persistency, but does not take a lot of effort once you get comfortable with your own routines. There is no right or wrong way to do it. You just need to do it.

46.

Manage Your Time, Don't Let it Manage You — Part III

I would consider myself a pack rat when it comes to holding on to information. However, I am realistic enough to know that I can't save everything. For example, I don't need every daily report saved. As part of my organizational improvement, I found I can't always be the controller of information—but I can know where and from whom to grab it. You should know who the key contact is for critical information. If you don't know who the key contacts are, you should invest the time to learn—it saves time in the end. How will doing more save you time? By making you more informed and effective, you will save time. Let's find out how.

To increase your effectiveness, you should read all of your emails and avoid the systemic rules for auto-deleting. If you need to set a rule to auto-delete the email (e.g., daily reports), don't bother getting the email in the first place. Also, read the entire email; don't just pull up the attachments or read the beginning. There are often key points in the body, or the email trail, that might need to be addressed. If you are one of the few reading the entire body of the email, you are in the minority—a minority that gives you an information advantage. Although there is etiquette to delete needless pieces of an email and to summarize when you are the person who forwards it or replies, we are realistic enough to know it doesn't always happen. Use the details to fully understand what is going on around you.

If there are attachments and you simply open them without reading the email, you may be missing out. There are often high-level summaries included in the email that provide context that will be extremely important as you pull up that attachment. Read the key points and the summary. This may save you time researching information that may already be in front of you.

Checklists are both a blessing and a curse. We have all used checklists.

Manage Your Time, Don't Let it Manage You—Part III

Some people use them better than others. Some people write out checklists chronologically, some people write out by priority, and some people write first come, first served (not recommended). Some people move the checklist from one day to another. If you are the daily shifter, stop using the checklist. Checklists are not productive if you constantly shift them from day to day—they simply become time wasters. If you have moved the same task for multiple days, how important is it? If it is important, take action on it. If it is important, but not urgent, don't schedule it for tomorrow; schedule it for a week from now when you know you can get to it. If you are proactively staying ahead of your day, your week, and your month as stated earlier, you should be on top of this anyway.

Checklists, if kept, must comprise the *least* amount of work you expect to get done and still consider the day a success. It might sound counterintuitive since we are trying to get the most out of a day. However, I specifically think of it as the, "I can't leave until this gets done" list. This should be your very realistic list. Anything finished after this list should be considered a bonus. Use a *pull* system to bring the bonus tasks into your freed up parts of your day as opposed to continually *pushing* the tasks to another day. You will start to find you will have a lot more bonus days as you get control of your checklists and calendar.

It is important with checklists to not write something down today if you are not going to do it today. In addition, you should double the time you expect to complete the tasks, even the regular ones, and account for interruptions (e.g., calls coming in, questions being asked, etc.). Doubling the time is critical for being realistic with time expectations.

The following are additional miscellaneous tips that will influence effective organization and time management:

- **How a request comes in may impact your time management.** How the requests are communicated to you play an important role when establishing priorities. Be cautious of email—it can be a time consumer if you are spending all day reading it and trying to interpret the exact request. You also increase the risk of multitasking. Use a specific block of time in a day to go through your emails and organize what is being asked of you. Additionally, pick up the phone and clarify the request, if needed, to avoid having to go back for rework.
- **Keep a copy of your calendar with you, even when not at your desk.** You can use an electronic/virtual version, print a smaller pocket version, or tape one in a notebook or portfolio you carry with you.
- **If possible, turn off the features that confirm you have a new email or messages.** Research has proven that it takes an inordinate amount of time to get back to your original thought when you are

The Transformation of a Doubting Thomas

interrupted—regardless of whether it is by email, text message, or someone asking a question. Additionally, don't pay attention to previews when an email comes in. It will naturally pull you to read the entire message and it takes away what you were previously dedicating your time toward. Turn off all indicators, whether it is visual or sound.

- **Touch it once.** Read it, take action, move it to a time when you can get to it, or save it for future reference. Stop moving it day to day because of an inability to take action; stop reading it more than once. Take actions on the emails—this might be moving it to another location or scheduling a meeting or a phone call, etc., to take it to its conclusion. Don't read an email and just leave it in your inbox. This causes you to read it multiple times.
- **I recommend not organizing emails by categories, senders, etc.** It takes away from your ability to see it once. This causes you to have to look into multiple places when researching or looking for something. I have rarely seen this work effectively without something falling through the cracks.
- **Give yourself some breathing room before you start your day so you are not rushed around.** It sets the tone for the day. Don't walk in the door at 7:59 A.M. if you are supposed to start at eight o'clock. That rushed feeling takes a while to go away.
- **Many of us have a tendency to do the easiest things first for the sense of accomplishment.** We must understand the difference between ease and true accomplishment. If you get a lot of easy things out of the way, after a while the more difficult things start to pile up. Also assess what is urgent, not urgent, important, and not important. Each of these needs to be reacted to in a different way. Do not give each a blanket reaction. Also, respect that what might be urgent or important to you may not be important or urgent to others. You should ask questions if you are unsure.
- **Ask what happens if the deadline if missed.** Know the rewards and consequences. You will be surprised how frequently what you thought of as urgent was really only important or vice versa, once clarity is added.
- **Understand that internal pressures are sometimes greater than reality.**
- **Always take a notebook to meetings and actually use it; then go back and refer to it.** Put any actions needed on your calendar.
- **Immediately file and organize—this includes paper, emails, and online filing, as needed. Don't pile up.**
- **If you have pushed the same task more than five days or made no progress on even starting on something, make a final decision on what

Manage Your Time, Don't Let it Manage You—Part III

action you need to take, including dismissing it. You do have options to take that immediate action: delete it, schedule time to address it, or take action to finish it now. A decision to do nothing is still a decision—just understand the consequences.

My former company used to consistently solicit people for their opinions regarding time management for certain roles. I used to laugh because the conclusions never changed. We used to conduct these time studies and came to the conclusion that there was not enough time in the day to get everything done. Don't wait for a time study to figure out what you do all day. Self-awareness will lead to your success. If you are feeling strained, you must discuss time management challenges with your manager. Silence will only hurt you. You must over-communicate with your manager regarding what's on your plate.

Time management is a requirement for all levels in an organization. If you don't have enough time to invest in improving your own time management, take another serious look. There are only twenty-four hours in the day. They should not be all devoted to work, but if you don't manage the work piece, you can't balance the personal piece. Start immediately.

47.

Don't Try to Boil the Ocean

The first time I ever heard the corporate jargon, "you can't boil the ocean," I was impressed with the simplicity and obvious nature of the statement. We have all bitten off more than we could chew at one time or another. I would think there are enough clichés related to this topic for all of us to get the point. However, we don't get the point. Whether we are in an effort to overachieve, trying to do too much, or trying to be the corporate hero, we all try to boil the ocean sometime.

There are a couple of key points. First, I have worked for managers who were unclear in their expectations of me relating to deliverables. The vagueness, or in some cases, vastness of the request was not realistic. I am all for stretch goals and the reach required to develop me while strengthening the business. However, if you're asked to solve world peace, and your manager wanted you to think globally and act locally, these are two different requests (I couldn't resist the additional cliché). The requester should have the end result in mind in order for the task to be fully understood and determined feasible. If the realistic nature of the end state is in question, refer back to the requestor. An assessment may be needed to determine if the request is even possible prior to investing too much into an unattainable request. However, the expectation needs to be clear that you are being asked for an assessment, not the ultimate end state.

Second, if you are the one doing the tasks, you can't take on the world by yourself all the time. If you try to boil the ocean by yourself, you will only succeed in increasing your frustration over time. I am a huge fan of small victories. I am not taking the easy way out, but I want you to be accepting of recognition for successful progression. The small victories will add up to many large wins. However, if you are constantly swinging for home runs, you may eventually hit one, but only after you strike out quite a few times. If you go for solid hits, and use the support system around you, you will all succeed as a team (I couldn't resist the

Don't Try to Boil the Ocean

baseball analogy). If you are the recipient of the grandiose "empty out the ocean" instructions, break it down into smaller parts. You need to also understand ultimately what the end result should look like. If you do not understand the expectations, ask clarifying questions until you get it.

Sometimes, managers aren't exactly sure what we are asking. Managers may pass down information that is filtered, and re-translated. It is your obligation to slow down the process enough for clear directions in order to increase satisfaction, improve production, and gain more wins by not boiling the ocean. If there is a big body of water in front of you, gather the team, resources, and invest the time required to confirm expectations needed to navigate through it. Far too many times, we attempt to do too much on our own. We can divide the responsibilities based on skill set, experience level, or many other ways. The point is the team can accomplish more with clear instruction and role clarity.

Our success is in our ability to know what is being asked of us and that we can't do it all on our own. The best leaders make sure they know what is being asked of them and don't do it by themselves. They surround themselves with a well organized team, delegate effectively, and play to everyone's strengths.

48.

Be Responsible With the Power of Position (P.O.P.)

Do you understand your true relationship with the people that work for you? If you are a manager of others, you are given power simply by having the title of manager next to your name. This title comes with great responsibility. Dr. Paul Hersey wrote in *The Situational Leader* that, "Power is influence potential. Power is the resource that enables a leader to gain compliance or commitment from others." Earlier in my career, I knew people "had" to listen to me because they reported to me, so I took advantage of it. I wasn't cocky or arrogant. I took advantage of what I thought were my responsibilities to provide feedback and make people better. The feedback pointed toward me at times was that I was often too direct and to the point. My intent was never to belittle, but to make my people better. I had not established a solid enough foundational relationship to be this direct. I was learning to be a manager, but I was not learning to be a leader.

I once walked into a new hire classroom and was asked a business-related question. My answer contradicted the trainer, who was not in the room. I instantly blurted out that she was wrong. The shocked looks on the newly hired employees said all that needed to be said. A so-called titled manager of this company had just taken away the respect that the trainer had been working so hard to gain. There were better ways to handle that situation. I could have said, "Let me check on that and get back to you," and discussed it with the trainer. Regardless of the final "right" answer, we both were in positions of authority in the eyes of the employees, and I abused my power and potentially adversely impacted the credibility of both myself and the trainer. I may have also left a lasting impression on the new employees' opinions about their decision to stay with the company. They may have asked themselves if all managers were like me.

Be Responsible With the Power of Position (P.O.P.)

Some people feared me. I grew to realize the fear wasn't because they would get yelled at. I made people feel badly for not performing at a level I thought they should be. I did not account for their individual circumstances, such as tenure, experience, and confidence. I would push everyone the same way, with the same intensity. This method worked for a few people, but not for most employees.

I followed policies to the letter of the law, and people did not see me as someone who would listen to all sides. I was their manager and not their leader. One day, I placed someone on corrective action for a customer situation. I based it on the side of the story I heard from others. When the person chose to supersede my authority and went to see my manager, I was upset that he had gone over my head. He told a completely different story from my interpretation. What I learned was that I thought I knew all of the answers, knew the policy, and had the authority to make the corrective-action decision. I soon found out I was missing facts and needed to listen more. When the situation settled down, I realized that I could have supported the employee by listening to his side prior to making any decisions. We all would have been better off. My manager gave me simple feedback that stuck with me: "You need to be sensitive to the power of your position." That day, I put a note on my desk that read, "P.O.P" to remind me every day of the power of my position.

Managers and leaders must decide how to effectively use the authority given to them when they start managing people. There are times when managers must make tough decisions to use their authority and position. However, everything is not about reprimanding. There are positive uses of authority, such as issuing rewards and recognition. What's important is the person in the position of power understands and assesses each situation as being unique.

A manager also may have the power of having more information at his or her fingertips than people may want or need. Managers have natural power that comes with the title and how they wield it becomes important in the eyes or their employees. Sometimes, I might just need the person to listen to me. If there is a fire in the building, that may not be the best time for a group discussion. However, I weighed too heavily in the past on this type of management style as a way to send my messages to employees about what to do, as opposed to them learning on their own or coming up the learning curve at their own pace. I had to understand how to adapt my style based on what was required at the time for the person, the situation, and me. This learning moment was critical to my own development, for my effectiveness as a leader, and for the earned respect of the people who worked for me.

The Transformation of a Doubting Thomas

Every move a manager makes is watched. As a manager, you are on stage whether you like it or not. You may not always be respected, but people feel the requirement to listen to you due to a fear of losing their job, repercussions to their job or responsibilities, or impacts to their compensation. You have the power of your position and must be careful in how this power is exercised. What kind of reputation do you have? I didn't know my reputation except for what was coming to me through focus groups and some feedback from my managers. I wish I had listened—I mean truly listened—because they were always accurate. Do you want respect because of the title, or do you want respect because of the work you and your team are able to accomplish? The power to move the business and gain the respect of the people around you is greater when that respect is earned and put to good use. We should make the effort to make the most of the influence we are given.

49.

Know When to Let Go and Move On (Get Over It)

As written earlier, I spend the thirty minute drive home from work analyzing my day to look for what went right. Unfortunately, I do have bad days. In these cases, I spend the time evaluating what I did wrong and what I could have done better. It is a good way to assess my performance and myself so that I can become better the next time. I'm sure my wife appreciates the wind-down time more than when I worked two minutes from the house. Unfortunately, I also have a habit of over thinking my day's assessment and continuing this far into the night. I overanalyze a lot of things, but there have been too many times when I have beaten myself up over things I should have just let go.

As a newer manager, I wondered why a solid performer of mine had been out of the office for a long time. I was getting worried about him and decided to call to make sure he was alright. We had a decent relationship and I felt comfortable making the call. When he picked up the phone, he said he was quitting. I asked if there was anything I could do to keep him. I was not looking for him to go into his health history, but I did want him to know that I cared and that I was there to help. He said that he was having a nervous breakdown and "no thank you" to the assistance. I thought the response was odd considering that he had never had any performance or conduct issues in the past.

He had always come to work with a smile on his face, ready to work, and gave no indication of any mental issues. However, I knew I was getting out of my psychiatric league, so I offered some internal services to help. He responded as if he was annoyed with my caring attitude. He said that I could not help, but if I truly wanted to know what was going on he would tell me. I was hesitant now, but if he wanted to get something off his chest, he could use me as a sounding board. He told me he had broken up with his girlfriend. Now, I personally was no expert on relationships

The Transformation of a Doubting Thomas

since I was single at the time, however, I knew it could sometimes be difficult. However, I did not think that most break-ups caused nervous breakdowns.

I thought I was being a good manager when I said he could use more time away from the office so he could work things out. He started to yell at me and said it was not possible to come back to work, ever. This was probably the time in the conversation to let things calm down, but I wanted to be the patient manager and be a good listener. The employee went on to say that his ex-girlfriend was the official voice on the prompt that every associate in the company heard at the introduction of every single phone call. This means that he would have had to listen to her taped introduction every time he answered a call—eighty times a day. I learned a lesson that day: sometimes you can't help, even when you want to. You can always try, but there are times when we just need to let go. I later found out the person did need professional help and there was not much I would have been able to do for him long term.

Sometimes, there are better things around the corner. You may recall my story about when I was not hired for a position in which I would have managed hundreds, but was given the opportunity to start a new task-force role to reduce employee attrition. Not being hired for the original role taught me the value of losing, but also taught the lesson to "get over it." I started to realize the many great things that are ahead of us when we let go and move on. Hard work and patience did pay off with a job I was better suited for, even though I did not know it at the time. The great news when I changed jobs was that I did not have to relocate my family, and I have since grown into several other, higher-level roles because of that particular stepping stone. For further validation that I was on a better trajectory, several years later, the economy crashed, the site I would have worked in closed, and the market we had been house hunting in dropped like a rock. I most likely would have been in financial trouble.

We have all had bad days or want something different. We may want to revisit a mistake, we may want a "do over," we may want to go back to the way things were, or may want what we can't have. I have to repeat three simple words: Get over it. Sometimes, our control over circumstances is limited. We need to deal with what we can, and learn to get over the rest.

I grew much happier when I began to understand that my career is not a sprint, it is a marathon that I hope grows and prospers with my ability to learn and become better. To use business jargon, if we continue to try to "die on this hill" or "spin our wheels," our attempts to move forward are hindered. If I am going to hang on too long to something, I should

Know When to Let Go and Move On (Get Over It)

make it the great days in my career. We should all play off the positive energy and momentum from the high points in our careers. We must take the appropriate time to recognize and celebrate the wins and enjoy them, learn from our trials, and get over the rest.

50.

Send Your Message to One Person and Watch it Grow

I can remember the many times I was sending a message to a group of people and wondered why the entire group didn't get it. Trying to swing the tide for a group of people is difficult at times. Although more of an investment needs to be made up front, I have found consistent success in my ability to make a difference by working with one person at a time, or with smaller groups of people. People learn in different ways, and at different speeds. Although larger group lessons—especially business-specific training—may save time, more difficult or complex messages may be better suited for one-on-one situations or smaller groups.

Additionally, in meeting situations, there are a variety of personalities, opinions, and experience levels. Not everyone in a room or a meeting is going to agree with what is being said, interpret what is being said the same way, or even engage in the same way. If you are trying to gain mutual buy-in for a new proposal, for example, you can gain an advantage in getting your points across more effectively if you have support already in the room. You can prepare by having conversations ahead of time with specific individuals. Even a quick conversation hitting key points reduces the surprise factor and will engage that person more in the conversation about the message you are trying to convey. If you feel there is going to be contention, it is much easier with support already on your side. Popular opinions grow when there is more support behind them. Your invested time prior to the meeting will not be wasted time; in fact, the invested time should make the meeting more efficient and effective by minimizing the arguments and contrary dialogue. I am realistic enough to know that the pre-meetings are not required for every meeting, but a targeted approach for key circumstances will be beneficial when there is a crucial message you want to convey.

I want to share a story about a message blossoming. I saw a résumé

Send Your Message to One Person and Watch it Grow

on a central printer in our workspace that was not organized well and contained multiple typographical errors. I decided to proactively contact the person and provide them feedback. I had experience in this field and wanted to make the story of her career stronger. I didn't know the person, but I wrote some notes and gave them to her manager to pass along. She came to see me and we went over the suggestions. The final product was excellent and one that made her burst with pride. She told some teammates about our interaction. I soon had a few more résumé conversations that turned into career direction conversations. I felt like a counselor, but I was enjoying the interaction and felt like each conversation was a learning experience for everyone. I was making a difference one person at a time. I became driven to help the people I was working with succeed. More often than not, they needed the little extra push to find their right path. I was learning that a positive message gets used and passed on.

In another example, I was invited to a small gathering to help spark interest in getting managers involved in developing themselves, developing their people, and getting more involved in the community. I shared many of my professional experiences, relating how my communication, confidence, and overall growth improved when I began to take steps to improve myself. I often mentioned Toastmasters as an opportunity for others to improve their communication and leadership skills. A few expressed interest in joining the group.

I was surprised when a senior leader whispered an invite to me to teach her managers how to more effectively manage up. I took the invitation and prepared an hour-long discussion. The small group interaction went well. A manager in another department had heard about it from one of the attendees and asked if I could teach his newer managers how to communicate more effectively. The session was expanded to include how to become more organized, how to network better, how to write résumés, and how to navigate through their careers. We turned the interactions into a monthly series, and the targeted audience was expanded to include more tenured managers and people from outside that particular line of business. Not one of these people reported to me, and not one of them was obligated to listen. I was learning to adapt my messages based on the audience, and was improving my ability to provide a message that people could walk away with and spread to others.

The next time you are finding little success in having your message absorbed, change your tack. You have important messages to send. Be proactive, patient, and creative. Pull someone to the side and watch the message spread.

51.

Become a Good Listener

Everywhere we look, people have headsets in their ears listening to music while the world goes on around them. I've seen people blindly walk into street poles as they are texting. We multitask more than we want and our attention span gets spread to the limit. We have side conversations with people in the room while a conference call is going on, check messages, or make a call in the middle of a conversation with someone. One of the more difficult things I've tried to learn is effective listening. I have to make a concerted effort to try to give my undivided attention to one person at a time. I have to emphasize that the operative word is *try*. This lesson is a constant work in progress. There are too many opportunities to pull my attention and focus somewhere else.

Effective listening is at risk of being a lost skill. I have found, however, that most successful decision makers and leaders have this rare ability to listen effectively. The ability to focus on one person at a time and truly hear what they have to say allows the whole story to be heard, and builds the relationship for more productive conversations in the future. Listening also builds trust and respect. Think of the person who is always interrupting you and speaking over you. I often found (all right, present tense: "find"—this is still a work in progress) myself doing this. I never had any intention to be rude, but had ideas swimming in my head that needed to be blurted out before they were forgotten or became irrelevant. Maybe I was attempting to be the smartest person in the room, trying to gain attention from my managers, or just wanted to be heard. When this happened, I was causing frustration and disruption to any real conversation, since the discussions were more one sided then they needed to be.

I had to force myself to listen and not speak. I thought I solved it by taking notes while someone else was speaking. However, I found that the notes started to dominate my own thoughts. I was still selfish in my approach to the conversation. I was silently interrupting someone's thoughts because, in reality, I wasn't truly hearing what they were saying. Many instances of speaking over people are caused by our need to share our next thought with the person we are talking to, regardless of what they are saying. That is really not a productive conversation.

I knew I was making progress when I entered the 2009 Fall Toastmasters International Speech Evaluation Contest. The goal of the contest is for all contestants to listen to the same "test" speech. The contestants can take notes during the speech and for five minutes immediately following, must organize and formulate their thoughts. The contestants then give a two to three minute overview "speech" of the key points they want emphasized for the "test" speaker and audience. I ended up finishing in second place in District 45, which includes over 100 clubs. I was using a critical ear, and more importantly, it was making a difference in my professional career.

I found significant improvement in my ability to have productive conversations and build more effective relationships when I put down my pen and simply listened to what someone said. I found there was a more open and fluid dialogue, and this generated more ideas and satisfaction on the part of the other person. Others involved in the conversations started to contribute, or at least felt the openness to contributing when they had something important to say. I found greater success personally and more productive teamwork simply by truly listening and not worrying about formulating my next thought.

True listening was a career-altering discovery for me. I still feel the pull, at times, to multitask or gather my next thought. However, the pull gets easier as I continue to practice this skill. The practice has taught me to be a more effective communicator all around because I am now more engaged in the conversation, since I am invited to ask open questions and clarify and confirm points. It is amazing the great things others have to say when I just started paying attention.

52.

Be the Bigger Person

I started working for someone who I felt talked behind my back and was making a major effort to push me out of his department. Remember the person who gave me *Don't Sweat the Small Stuff*? Prior to him joining our department, I had been put into a temporary position managing managers and felt I was on my way to a promising future. My bad feelings were confirmed after his arrival a little over a year later when I was removed from my position and asked to take a step back. My backwards movement was to some degree a self-fulfilling prophecy, because I was not motivated to work for him. However, I also could not seem to break through to find what it would take for him to change his mind.

Although I was not motivated to give him my best, I did try to hide my outward frustration by burying my head in my work. My goal was to work as hard as I could until something changed (e.g., the "Wait three months" mentality). I knew he was under a lot of pressure to perform, but I had the opinion that he spent too much time trying to impress the upper management for his next promotion versus running his own business well. I had some small wins, but I knew we would never find the mutual respect needed to succeed as a team.

We crossed paths a few times over the years and I still boiled over with frustration that he never seemed to respect my work. Years later, I ended up working for him a second time. We had both matured. I saw the relationship dynamic changing because he was not working for the same people he had always been trying to impress. A situation presented itself in which he needed my experience and job knowledge in his new department. He gave me more responsibilities and the space to succeed. He allowed me the chance to lead a task force of over one hundred people in a completely different area, with a lot of reign in directing our road map to success.

Our professional respect seemed to be growing. However, the entire tenure of the second round always seemed to have an eight-hundred pound gorilla in the room. It was the frustration from our first go-around together. We should have had a sit down conversation and put it all out on the table. We didn't do that. We worked better together in this new partnership, but there was still so much more we could have accomplished if we had just hammered out our differences, or at least gotten over the past.

Soon after the merger, he left the company. I was actually the last person to see him in the hall on his last day. He asked if I would help him take a box from his office to his car. I had a quick thought of, "I can't believe he still wants to put me to work." However, I knew that wasn't his true intention and he just needed a little assistance. Believe it or not, he did have an underlying motivation—even with the impromptu run in with me. As we were walking out, he said, "I'm sorry." He went on to talk about all of the pressures he had been under during our first time together and how he had wanted to climb the corporate ladder as quickly as possible, even if it meant stepping on people. He was confessing his own learning to me and confirming that my original opinions weren't too far off.

I realized that if I had taken the first step by stating my opinion years ago, I could have avoided a lot of the uncomfortable feelings we'd had. He took the first steps and told me all the great things he appreciated about me and the respect he had gained from my ability to work through the difficulty he had put me through. I felt guilty for not making the first move, but was proud of my ability to force my way through the hard times. I also gained a lot of respect for him for taking advantage of the current events to make a difference in our relationship.

I know it has a lot of similarities to a death bed conversation we would have wanted to hear earlier in our lives from that person. However, I had the luxury of still living in a small New England town with this individual. Our interactions in town are cordial and personable. He ended up getting a new job in one of our old buildings right up the road. I was driving home and passed his building on a Friday afternoon. We stopped and talked. He needed leadership help in his new business and asked if I would join. I did not take him up on it, but carried the valuable lesson of what can become of being the bigger person.

53.

Surround Yourself With Pictures

I once went to a work seminar on organization. One of the suggestions the instructor made was to not have any pictures around you. The premise was that the pictures can cause distractions. Since this class took place during my first few months of being a manager, I took it seriously. I even mentioned the concept to people who had pictures on their desks and suggested they remove them. I didn't win a whole lot of points with these suggestions, but I did practice what I preached. I spent years with a desk devoid of pictures because I didn't want to be distracted. For the most part, I didn't feel distracted, so I reasoned that it must be working. What I failed to realize at the time was that I was not married, did not have any pets, or children, so I was not actively looking to put too many pictures on my desk anyway. I was fully dedicated to the company.

About five years later, I got married. I had the first picture dilemma. Did I put a picture of my wife up on my desk? She was beautiful and special, and I couldn't resist. I was going to take the chance and see if I truly was distracted. We got a black Lab to add to the family. One of my favorite pictures of all time came a couple years later. It was a picture of my first born daughter in a tide pool with our dog looking over her. My family grew over the next few years with two more beautiful daughters entering my life. I never stopped putting pictures up of my family and dogs, pictures of celebrated work events, and friends.

I had motivation. I had people to work hard for and support. I could look at their pictures and see a smile when I was having a bad day. When I needed advice, I could look toward my wife's picture and know exactly what she would think and suggest (I did not, however, get to the point of talking to my pictures). I never felt distracted once. I felt moved and driven to push harder to make sure they all had what they needed from me. The harder and smarter I worked, the more I could provide for them. As the years have gone on, I see my babies growing up into young ladies.

Surround Yourself With Pictures

These young ladies will grow up to become adults someday and be successful in whatever their hearts desire. I know I can't stop now. The pictures show me how quickly they grow and change and keep me motivated every day.

Although it took years for me to figure it out, pictures add a new dimension to my work space. They bring the comfort of home, and lend familiarity and stability when you might need it most. Surround yourself with pictures of good times with family and friends. I was given a digital frame and immediately loaded it with over one thousand photos. I periodically turn around and chuckle when I see a picture flash up that brings back great memories. The pictures don't distract me. The pictures motivate me because they are of the people who mean the most to me.

54.

Get to Know the People You Work With

There are far more people I have managed whose names I can't remember than people whose names I can. Besides having a poor memory with names (I'm working on it), the key driver is the fact that I did a poor job early in my career of getting to know the people I worked with as real people. I knew them as employees. I knew their statistics, the way a baseball manager might know his players. I knew their tendencies. I knew their strengths, and their potential to improve.

As I changed teams or people came and went, I would pick up on the statistics and begin the exercise to get to know the new numbers. I had failed to truly get to know the people I worked with. I once had a senior leader say, "Us being friends is merely a convenience." He meant that our personal relationship was not important. Since I had heard this prior to being a manager, I took it seriously and was self-driven to find my way to get to the next level. Once I became a manager, I steamrolled through the people I worked with to drive them to maximize their statistics the way I had when I was in their shoes just a few months before.

I did not get to know the people who worked for me at a personal level. As their manager, I was missing part of each of my employees' stories. If I had learned the value of knowing the personal side of people early in my manager experience, I would have known what makes a person tick. I could have adapted my feedback to better meet their style, gain more buy-in, and probably gain their respect. We would have had more to talk about and I could have built up our relationship. Instead, we simply talked statistics and I would ask, "How was your weekend?", although I really didn't want a real answer to the question. I was missing a chance to become a more effective leader and, more importantly, I was missing a chance to get to know the people to build a lasting relationship that would assist in everyone's growth—mine included.

I have matured enough to learn to get to know the people I work with better. We have personal conversations. I ask pointed questions about their pets, kids, or spouse. I remember things better because I have been more engaged in the conversation. I like the people better, because I actually know them. I had gone too long being professionally driven. I was given the unfortunate advice, "We do not have to be friends to succeed." I didn't go to work to make best friends. However, we all need relationships in our lives. If you nurture these relationships, everyone wins. If you happen to get a good friend out of the deal, then you will be better off. If you happen to only strengthen a working relationship, then the organization and both individuals are still better off.

Leaders flexible enough to tailor their styles to each individual's drivers and motivators are an asset to any company. I am now in a much better position to motivate the people who work with me because I understand what inspires them to come to work each day. In fact, many times, I simply ask the question, "Why do you come to work every day?" There is nothing like getting straight to the point. Now, I know whether the person is working because of family, pride, money, promotions, or simply a pat on the back.

55.

Balance Being a Leader and a Doer— You Can't Do Both at the Same Time

On my mentor and networking monthly rotation, there was a question I asked of two leaders who had some familiarity of my background and reputation. I asked, "What would it take to get to the next level?" since I felt all of my recent moves were lateral. I was surprised to hear similar answers from these two respected leaders. I was told that I had a reputation of being the "clean up guy." I was the one willing to get in the trenches and find the issues that needed to be fixed. I was independent in my thinking and did not need a whole lot of direction. I could execute whatever task needed to be done. I took these comments as a compliment. The comments were really intended to inform me that I was good at what I was doing as a "doer," but the question remained: What was I doing to prove that I was a leader? There is nothing wrong with being a doer; there is always significant need in every business for someone to come in and diagnose and improve. However, there is a distinction between a "doer" and a "leader" and I wanted to explore how to be the latter.

There were a couple of points being made. First, I continued to accept new positions at a lateral level, so the consensus was that I enjoyed project management and that I could execute on the deliverables. Second, I had not adequately built up the reputation that I could lead when given more complex job responsibilities. The job always got done when I was there, but that was because I had a tendency to step in and start doing it myself. I was not leading a team or project; I continued to be in the way as the doer, or in team situations the micro-manager and meddler. It is all right to want control of every detail, but this can cause frustration within a team. In addition, it had the potential of sending a message that I did not trust my people. It always crushed the creative juices of the collective group if I simply pushed my own agenda onto them or moved them out

Balance Being a Leader and a Doer—You Can't Do Both at the Same Time

of the way. Both mentors told me to set clear expectations, and then get out of the way of the team. I had the skills and potential to be a leader, but first I had to stop being the doer, especially when I was the supposed leader.

I was involved in a leadership program that diagnosed and identified my certain tendencies as a leader. To no one's surprise, I found that I liked to roll up my sleeves and get dirty. We were asked to lead an initiative and play toward our weaknesses. I had identified a project that needed to be implemented. I assembled an extremely strong team, identified a competent project manager, and watched from the sidelines. I made myself available for periodic updates and attempted to eliminate road blocks. With clenched fists and a constantly bitten lip, I watched everything unfold in front of me. I allowed the process to run its due course. The leader did a phenomenal job. The project was completed on time and had greater business impacts than originally projected. I was able to allow the team to present their findings and recommendations to the senior leaders. All the while, I was there for support, suggestions, and debate. Although I had the most experience and job knowledge, I remained silent for the most part and allowed the team to shine. My name was listed as the project leader, and that's who I wanted and needed to be. I successfully lead the project team members and was finally not a doer.

The first thing that was said to me after the presentation was how smoothly this had run and how much we accomplished as a team. The senior leaders praised me for being such an active leader in driving the process. It had always seemed counterintuitive to let others do the work because it may not turn out exactly as I had envisioned, but it made more sense now that I'd experienced it in action. I could be detailed-oriented, I could be intelligent about my business, and I could be there to lead the business. I did not have to be a micro-manager and watch every detail if I built the right team and set the right expectations. I needed to take accountability for the final project, but if I did my job right, the success for the project would take care of itself with a more satisfied team and a better end result. I learned that I can't be the leader and the doer at the same time.

56.

Give People Second Chances

I always seemed to wind up working for people who looked out for me and were willing to give me second chances. Even as I griped about my managers and blamed them for many of my downfalls, I was still asked to go with them as they changed jobs within my company. In a corporation employing thousands of people, I had many years in which I seemed to work for people willing to give me second chances at a time in my career when I thought I was making too many mistakes. I thought, at times, that they were protecting me. What I found was that these special managers were not protecting me—they were willing to give me a second chance because they knew my strengths better than I did. Over the years, as I gained confidence and learned more about the business on my own, they saw my maturity even before I did. The people who gave me a second chance knew I would give everything I had for the business, and knew I was learning from my mistakes. Additionally, I was learning to own up to my mistakes and was making it an active practice to teach others by sharing what I had learned from my lessons.

In one of my first positions managing managers, I was new and naïve to the role. I was previously a micromanager and I had stayed steadfast to personnel policies. When I should have been a level higher than where I was in order to manage managers, I was really a glorified version of a manager because I knew the technicalities of the business but did not understand how to manage it.

My manager invested his time with me, as I was new to the role. He had a certain tone he used when I made mistakes, but sought to make them teaching opportunities. I still couldn't break out of the glorified manager mentality, even though I was supposed to be a level higher. Mistakes were made, and we both felt I was not coming up the learning curve quickly enough. However, he made the effort to make me better and gave me opportunities even though I was convinced I had not reached his

Give People Second Chances

expectations. When he left the department, I appreciated his time and dedication, and told him I would continue to make the effort to improve.

I was a little surprised when I got a call to join him in his new department. I had previously worked in that department and could bring my job knowledge. But why would he want me when he knew exactly what I was—and was not— capable of? I'm now convinced that that was why he made the call to me. He knew exactly what I could and could not do, and he still saw the potential.

I thought then that I was still too naïve to truly lead the department, since I needed to develop my own confidence level. I began to think that I was being harder on myself about being perfect than I needed to be, but I still lacked confidence. I was surrounded by tenured peers who I let take control of meetings and drive the conversations. My confidence was not growing, but my frustration was.

If you recall from the "Set an Example" chapter, we had an annual event that was supposed to be fun, I did not engage in the event as much as I should have. My avoidance of the event, which was supposed to include tasteful practical jokes, only caused more unwanted attention directed my way. As a result, I became an unwilling target. I felt an obligation to defend myself and my team and went on the offensive halfway through the month, after giving in to the pressure to participate. My team and I devised some creative practical jokes that walked a fine line of professionalism and ultimately landed me in hot water with Human Resources. I pushed the limits out of frustration rather than simply playing along from the beginning.

Whatever frustrations I had with the event remained bottled up until my manager had to sit me down and explain his concerns about my actions. I let it all out, including my disdain for the event, my growing disrespect for my peers, and the fact that I felt forced into doing things I was not comfortable with. I came to the realization that I was the only one accountable to make the decision to do what I had done. I didn't think through the unintended consequences and the impact I would have on my team and my peers. I vented and he listened, then we had a phenomenal conversation. The conversation was straightforward and should have occurred prior to allowing the frustration to build up.

As much as I was embarrassed that we had to have the HR discussion, I needed it. I maintained my job with a solid slap on the wrist, and learned some lessons. However, I was not convinced that I would ever work for this person again, since it was a pretty big mistake in my eyes relating to people management.

As is the nature of our business, he moved on to another department.

The Transformation of a Doubting Thomas

I received another call six months later. He wanted me to work for him again in a department that was full of newer managers. I jumped at the chance because I wanted to prove myself to him, and I saw an opportunity to teach all of my new peers to avoid my past mistakes relating to people management. I saw my chance to give back and be the leader I wanted to be. For three months, I was able to accomplish this and a lot more. I felt like I had made a name for myself in this new department and that I was there making a difference. I was asking questions and driving the business. My questions landed me in a three-month task force that lasted for over two years. Guess who joined me after I left his department, two days later? You guessed it—he moved to my new department as my manager, again. He apparently had had some inkling as to his next move and wanted me to be there with him. He knew exactly what he was getting, and he seemed pretty happy to know who had his back.

Through my career, I've sometimes perceived that I've been in the wrong place at the wrong time, and sometimes I've felt that I've been in the right place at the right time. I was learning to go with the flow and learn from my mistakes. I also learned to give second chances. As a perfectionist, I know that no one, including myself, is perfect. We can all strive to do our best. I have always been appreciative of people willing to give me tough feedback, even when I didn't think I wanted to hear it. I became a manager known for openly sharing my mistakes to help others. In fact, a few times when I thought my people were holding back out of fear of making mistakes, I started a regular event in our weekly staff meetings to share our "MOW: Mistake of the Week." We shared what we had learned through the week and found that we all made mistakes. We were willing to take calculated risks, work together as a team, and be more creative. I now actively recruit people I know have made mistakes, who are willing to own them and learn from them. I have found that giving people second chances only strengthens the team and the individual's efforts.

57.

Do Stuff You Love

There are two thought processes when it comes to career movement and development within a corporation. First, you should become an expert in your field and hone your trade so you are the go-to person. Businesses are in need of in-depth expertise—specialists. If a business is in constant flux with transitioning people from place to place, there will be instability and constant learning curves that may be steep. The second opinion is one in which you are in a constant learning mode and moving from one place or another. If your company is large enough, you have the opportunity to move throughout the organization to broaden your depth of knowledge—generalists. This thought process is about bringing your expertise with you from the past areas to come up with creative and fresh ideas for your new area. I averaged about eighteen months per position prior to eventually moving on. There have been very few times when I said I had learned everything I ever needed to know where I was, and there are fewer times when I could say that there was nothing to learn or share in the new position.

Businesses need both types of leaders—specialists and generalists—in their organization. Companies need people who know the business intimately and people who have a broad base across multiple aspects of the business to give it perspective. The decision within a corporate culture about moving or staying is up to company expectations, and as importantly, it is up to what the individual wants. Personally, I seem to thrive as a generalist, but that has been a choice. I have rarely been bored in any of my roles, but I find I also get an itch to continue to learn different pieces of the business. Even when I went back to previous departments, I was typically in a new role and the business had changed significantly. I moved with my family multiple times as a child to many states because of my dad's job. I guess moving around so many times growing up made it seem natural to be in a constant state of change with new positions. I was

The Transformation of a Doubting Thomas

flexible and eager for all new challenges.

What is important is that you love what you do and do stuff you love. Whether you are doing many different things or the same thing each day, you should love it. There will be bad days, frustrating days, and days you may think will never end. However, regardless of what your motivation is to go to work every day, can you find something about your job you like? Whether you like the challenge of finding solutions to problems or enjoy the people you work with, there needs to be some piece of what you do that you love. I love the different learning experiences. I love the challenge of fixing problems. I enjoy the people I work with (most of the time). I love that I was never pigeon-holed into one spot.

I wouldn't want anyone to regret never trying something different career-wise after doing the same thing and going to the same desk for twenty-plus years. I have talked to too many people who want to try new and different things—they need variety. As someone who studied people retention, and just being an observer of those around me, there are some employees who are miserable where they are and need a change. With the understanding that some people are just hanging onto their jobs for a paycheck, and the economy may dictate openings in a field, if you have the chance to choose, take advantage of it. Let me make it clear that people always have a choice to leave. There may be some timing constraints, or other mitigating factors that hold you back, but there shouldn't be twenty years when you didn't have some type of opportunity to grow or make a decision to move on. You have choices to make the job something you love or to move into something else that you will love.

As an employee you should be proactive in finding out about the overall business and understand what gets your interests and juices flowing. If you look around and find that what you are doing is still great, guess what—you found something you love. If you find other places where you feel you can make a difference or want to learn about that aspect of the business, approach someone. Let people know what your interests are. I never went to school to be a banker. In fact, I did what I could to avoid numbers. I've had positions where I was a business analyst, where I managed reporting and incentives, oversaw certain aspects of the budget, and used all of my skills. I am a banker now and have no plans to leave banking. I am fascinated everyday about how much there is to banking, whether it is credit cards, ATM and debit cards, mortgage, financing, savings, checking, and investments. I love what I do. When I didn't love what I was doing at any given time, after I gave it ample time to fully grasp my satisfaction level, I pursued other things. I often joke with my managers that I can't keep a job. I'm not sure if people are kicking me

Do Stuff You Love

out or if I am a wanted person. In either case, I have typically landed on my feet in a place where I made a difference; in a place I loved to work.

58.

Share Best Practices

I once managed a team of about fifteen people who were situated next to another team about the same size. We were starting up a new business on site. It was exciting times and we recruited and hired the best and the brightest people. My peer on the other team and I made the unspoken decision to not share our ideas or best practices with each other. We were both stubborn and competitive, and we were most likely hoarding our knowledge and team ideas to help ourselves look better in the eyes of our manager in the hopes of advancing ourselves. I guess this was an effort to step on each other on the way up the corporate ladder.

We sat in the same staff meetings and were often eager to share our team successes with our manager, but we never sat down together, just the two of us, to share ideas that made our new department successful. We knew one another's team statistics and rankings as much as our own team's results. However, we never did anything together to build cohesion among the overall group, including mutual meetings or team events unless specifically directed by our manager.

When the focus group feedback came in, it was miserable for both of us. We were perceived as non-team players and our rationale was shrouded in mystery as to why we made such an effort to separate the teams. The focus group desperately wanted team events, even as simple as food days. They couldn't figure out why we seemed to get along with each other but held back on creating an environment in which everyone wanted to work together. What was interesting was that we enjoyed each other's company, but allowed the passive-aggressive competitiveness to get the best of us when we were working together.

The employees were confused, the teams suffered, and the new business suffered from our poor leadership. Neither one of us found the fast track up that corporate ladder we so desperately fought each other over. Competition is a great motivator when used correctly, and can be used

Share Best Practices

to sustain performance. Two managers lacking the ability to build cohesion who negatively impact motivation do not create the most conducive environment to share best practices, or inspire people to perform.

The focus group feedback threw the cold water on our faces we both deserved. The next steps were easy. We invested time together on a routine basis, and made it obvious to everyone that we were on the same team. We shared our focus group feedback details and the actions we were planning to do to fix the issues. The manager was impressed. The teams came together. We had more ideas generated from the combined effort. The competition didn't go away, but it was more targeted and more fun. We began to set the bar even higher when we competed against other regions doing the same job function, and set the tone and performance bar for the company. We both learned a valuable lesson that two (or more) heads are much better than one. We continued to work together and saw the value of our efforts once we realized that there was plenty of room for both of us to advance. If that wasn't the case, then it would be because the best person earned it. We knew that each of us were now considered a great team player and others would see our value soon enough.

Years later, we both continued with our successful careers, both still learning all the way. We crossed paths often, and when we didn't, we called each other periodically to ask questions and share information. In fact, we met recently and discussed ideas about a new role that he was interested in. He ended up getting an executive position, and I was very proud of him. Best practices strengthen the core of the team, ensure the competency of everyone around you, and assist in building the capabilities of an ever-changing business model.

This book is my concerted effort to share many best practices I have picked up over the years. Most are not original, or even earth-shattering creative ideas. I have learned that I do not have to be the creator of the idea; I just need to be the one to move it forward and pass it on. Even when giving proper credit to the creator, I am often thanked for taking the time to share with others. Be a team player and don't let individual goals or the wrong motivation drive the wrong behavior. You may find short term gains by withholding information, but it will eventually hurt you individually, and it is not good for the overall business. This doesn't mean "nice guys finish last". It does means that you can get there together. There is enough space on the podium for those who share their ideas.

59.

Take Time for Yourself—You Deserve It

We say we need to work hard, work smart, do more with less, and burn the midnight oil. It is physically and mentally not feasible to keep doing it over and over without some type of break. Remember when the idea was for all the new technology—such as mobile devices and the Internet—to make our jobs easier and allow us to spend more time with friends and family? It turns out that the new technology adds to our ability to constantly connect with work. Besides the fact that cell phones have somehow created a new breed of louder talkers in airports, it has also allowed work to creep into our personal lives and blur the line between personal and professional time.

We all want to do well, possibly advance, and get confirmation from our boss that we are doing well. Some people like to send emails with a late night timestamp to create the question, "What were you doing working at midnight?" However, burning the midnight oil will cause burn out. Our jobs are important. So are family and friends. Don't forget that.

We all deserve a break from work. In the short term, do something for yourself, like walking away from the desk. Grab lunch, clear your head, and get a little breather. In the long term, take the vacation you have earned and enjoy it without checking in to the office. You should spend time with your friends and family to unwind. When I talk about unwinding, I mean turning off all connections to the office. Believe it or not, the business will run without you. Although there is no such thing as eight to five anymore, you have to recharge. It is good for you and it is good for the business. If you have established the right relationship with your boss and set the right expectations for your team, you might even gain more respect as your team shows off what you have taught them.

You don't want to say later in life, "I wish I didn't miss that event with my kids." I feel like I did early in my career. I have gone back and thought about the things I missed. I have had difficulty trying to remember why

Take Time for Yourself—You Deserve It

I wasn't there. Was it a "critical" meeting? Most times, I can't remember. When I do the opposite and remember the kid's events I have attended, I can't remember what I missed at work. It tells you something. The business will run without me, whether I truly believe it or not. In fact, if I do my job well, it *should* run smoothly without me. I have built up enough trust in the people doing the job in my absence. I will cover for them when they are out, and we both get the ability to recharge our batteries. For those people who think they are the only ones who can do their job, most times they are wrong. Hoarding responsibility only creates stress for those depending on you and creates stress for you as the sole owner. When you leave for what you may call a vacation, it probably isn't as relaxing as you want it to be. If you leave the impression that you not being in the office will leave huge holes if you can't be contacted, you are creating a potentially harmful dependency. Creating this type of dependency is not good for anyone. You have to make a concerted effort to create independency for your sanity.

Give in to the fact that you work hard (and smart), and you will take the time to enjoy it. None of your family and friends needs to watch you continuously on your cell phone while you should be with them, and you are most likely not engaged in whatever is happening anyway. The point of time away from work is to enjoy yourself, the people around you, and to relax—you deserve it.

60.

Get Involved at Work, at School, or at Life and Find Out How Contagious It Is

I have to admit that I participated in the obligatory walk-a-thons, bowl-a-thons, and everything-else-a-thons because I was asked—or told in some cases—to attend. I worked for a company that encouraged involvement in the community and helping others, almost to a fault. I felt forced, at times, to participate. Many times, I just went through the motions. I donated money to causes and donated my time based on whichever path the company took me. My heart was not in it early in my career because, selfishly, I did not see what was in it for me. I saw many smiling faces from appreciative people and saw large amounts of money raised to help special causes. However, I could not see, yet, what I got out of those events.

After I got married, I watched my incredible wife selflessly give up her time and effort to help out children, neighbors, communities, and schools. All were done unconditionally and with an admirable eagerness. I, again selfishly, did not appreciate her efforts all the time and found myself getting upset when she would invest significant amounts of her time to a cause I did not truly understand. I had yet to identify with the contagious nature of voluntarily getting involved. I mean getting involved not because I was told I should, but because others needed the helping hand and it was the right thing to do.

We have a company dedicated to helping developmentally challenged individuals right across the street from my house. I slowly started to understand the meaning of some of the smiles on my neighbors' faces when my wife spent a lot of her time helping to raise money for their facilities. They, in turn, went through a daily ritual to feed my dog biscuits. It was comical and hit a chord with me. My message here is to not necessarily find the one cause and dedicate all of your time (although this is a great option). The message is to find a place in your heart where the unconditional aspects of your involvement come flooding out.

Get Involved and Find Out How Contagious It Is

My first real taste of pure enjoyment in volunteering came when I was asked to participate in a small town group of people interested in bringing the sport of lacrosse to our community. I had played in high school in Pennsylvania at a time when there were approximately twenty teams playing in the entire state. My high school coach learned the game from clinics and from a book he carried in his back pocket. He dedicated his time to teaching us something we all grew to love. We weren't very good, but we became a team of great friends, learned about sportsmanship, and were able to give a virtually unknown local sport a little attention.

The new volunteer group created a nonprofit organization, received donated equipment, and held clinics for young kids. I had a blast for the year of my involvement. When I taught the younger kids how to play, I saw a look on their faces that showed me how excited they were to begin something special. Less than five years later, the effort grew to a club team at the high school level, prior to becoming a varsity program for boys and girls. As my kids grew older, I started to assist with the youth soccer programs. The pure enjoyment of watching kids learn and play an organized event is unbelievably contagious.

On the work front, I previously noted that I joined Toastmasters International to boost my own résumé. Part of my reasoning was the pull to get more involved in newly developed groups at work. Toastmasters was one of a few new clubs that came as an offshoot of a small group of grassroots leaders from the company who felt we had to do more on site. The goal of this grassroots group was to advance diversity and get more people involved in things they believed in. I knew that I could lead the new Toastmasters group after it had stalled for almost a year since originally being chartered.

The company encouraged Toastmaster's participation, so I knew it would be a positive step for me professionally. I was almost instantly obsessed with the start-up Toastmasters operation. I was amazed at how quickly people started to get caught up in the benefits of Toastmasters. There were multiple people who were hesitant to even show up as guests, let alone stand up in front of a group of people. Yet, when they did, their mistakes turned into learning, which turned into greater confidence in ability. I saw people who said over thirty "um's" and "ah's" in their first four-minute speech, provide a perfectly organized and formulated seven-minute speech with proper grammar (and no filler words) less than three months later.

Toastmasters challenged my abilities to effectively balance work, family, and other obligations. I found, with smart planning, that I could do them all effectively. My wife unconditionally supported every move

The Transformation of a Doubting Thomas

I made with the club. I started to emerge as a respected leader on the work campus, and I found that my communication skills improved and were getting noticed. I was getting something out of it, but that was no longer my sole motivation to be there. I saw the value of teaching others and watching them gain self confidence. Because of Toastmasters, I even wrote a speech about my first visit to the Maine State Special Olympics that turned into befriending the company's Special Olympic team and becoming a committed volunteer.

Our Toastmasters club had an active military person who had presented his manager with a prestigious national award. He was embarrassed for himself and knew he could improve his presentation skills. He joined our group and went after his personal goal to achieve his communication certification with fervor and impatience. He had a lust to learn and improve. He was called to active duty and brought his Toastmasters manuals with him and still pursued his goals to get certified. He was the third person in the club to achieve this certification. He achieved his own personal goals, and I burst with pride watching the drive to accomplish something that meant so much to him and his family.

I saw people in our club get involved in order to build up their leadership and communication skills, and then became successful club officers. The club grew from the original two people to a fairly consistent level of twenty five members in less than eighteen months. Our club partnered with other internal work groups to assist them with their communication and leadership skills, and soon we found ourselves expanding beyond our original vision. I joined for myself, and found myself staying for others. It was contagious.

61.

Know the Whole Story

I have had far too many examples of instances when I allowed my emotions—such as frustration—to dictate my mood, my decisions, and my interactions. There have been plenty of times when I needed to practice one of Steven Covey's *7 Habits of Highly Effective People* and "seek first to understand, then to be understood." You can't reinforce this enough in both the workplace and at home. I thought I would share a personal experience to illustrate how easy the concept is and how conscientious we need to be to practice it.

I have a neighbor of over eighteen years with whom I rarely had any issues. We are not close, but have a cordial relationship. He has been a good and helpful neighbor. He does, however, have a dog that I have often worried about when it was near my kids. Admittedly, the dog has never barked loudly enough to scare me, charged after anyone or anything that would have caused my angst. Instead, I didn't like the look or the breed, and simply had a bad feeling about it.

Late one night, the dog was out in his yard barking loudly. It was atypical and was getting on my nerves. The barking and whining wouldn't stop and went on for many hours. I was tired and cranky, and I couldn't sleep. Yet, I didn't do anything to check on it or fix the problem. It became obvious that my neighbor was not home so in my eyes there was no one to call; I guess it was just easier to stew over the situation and periodically complain to my wife.

After hours of this barking, my wife couldn't stand it any longer and walked across the yard in the dark. The dog was tangled and stuck, and was calling in its own special way for help. Although I had a predisposed nasty and angry attitude about this dog before this event, it was only exasperated as the barking continued. My wife quickly understood the situation, untangled the dog, provided him water, and said he was the sweetest thing. We later found out that another neighbor was supposed to let him

The Transformation of a Doubting Thomas

out and had forgotten.

    I'm sure that there are more professional examples that I could share, but the innocence of an animal made this example stand out. We need to fully understand situations prior to judging and overreacting to them. There are more sides to a story than just our own.

62.

Be Yourself — the Paradox

Dress to impress. You are told you are constantly onstage and people are constantly paying attention to you. Your manager is watching your every move. Now, just try to be yourself. We panic and get uptight when our boss's boss asks for something. Thoughts go through our mind, such as, "Will this be good enough for them?", "I need to impress them," and "What do I need to do to get noticed?" When we have senior leaders visit our building, everyone seems to panic. Messages go out to clean up the work areas, and all of a sudden our business-casual dress code goes away and the ties come back out. If the suits and ties aren't on, there are at least blue blazers everywhere.

I used to wonder if I didn't get that last promotion because my shirt was wrinkled that one time. I now can't remember what I wore yesterday, let alone keep track of everyone else. This isn't about how you dress, it is about how you present yourself…everyday. You shouldn't put on an act just because there are special guests. In fact, what message does that send to people who work for you and work with you if you suddenly change? There are higher ranked people out there, so what? The key is to find your personality and be consistent with it. If you like to create a fun-looking environment with decorations all around, why can't your upper management see it? If you made the decision to put it up, why can't it stay up? If you maintain a clean and safe environment all of the time, there shouldn't be a panic the night before someone comes. I learned to rarely fret over my environment because I maintain it on a regular basis and attempt to teach everyone the importance of presenting themselves respectfully everyday, anyway.

I had to learn to stop trying to impress everyone, all the time. I wanted to take care of my manager, take care of my peers, and take care of the people who worked for me. I wanted to be everywhere, all the time, and give everyone what they wanted when they wanted it. I got

The Transformation of a Doubting Thomas

disappointed in myself if my boss requested changes or offered suggestions. I took it personally because they were not impressed with my work. I found I tensed up during presentations, used words that were not natural to me, and tended to be over the top in making the effort to ensure that I was noticed.

When we were in the midst of my former company being bought out, I had a choice to work harder and impress more people, or just do my job to the best of my ability. I was concerned about the unknown, but had confidence in my own ability. I found that the stress of this transition brought out personalities I had never seen before. I saw selfishness in some people who wanted all of the glory, I saw people give up, and I saw people who I thought had loyalty to the company turn their heads. It was an interesting time for everyone. However, the ones who impressed me the most were the ones who never changed along the way. I learned a valuable lesson about the importance of being myself. What did I have to worry about? I was comfortable in my own skin and my confidence had been growing. I was always commended for my hard work, so what needed to change? I had feedback given to me on how to improve, and the only challenge I now had was how to implement the feedback and still be myself. I began to understand how I could do that.

I can't tell you how much more satisfied and content I was with my job and the company when I let down my guard enough to be Tom Dowd. I was not Tom Dowd the Banker, or Tom Dowd the Manager, or Tom Dowd (place label here). I was starting to be more engaging and had more personal conversations to get to know people. It wasn't wasting time like I had always thought in the past. I could carry a conversation and I could also balance it with my business needs. I was relating to people, because they were starting to relate to me.

I could attend my child's play, concert, or game on my own terms because I wanted to be there, because I was being myself, knowing that the job would get done. I was building a stronger bond with the people I worked for and worked with, because they knew exactly what they were getting with me. I had the confidence to know what needed to be done at work and when it had to be done. If there was a conflict, I used my strong relationships to talk to my manager about it. I would instill in them enough confidence to know the job would get done, whether it was by delegating or working different hours. That's not trying to impress, that's just getting your job done the right way.

I have never whipped my cell phone out to look busy in the hall, and have never intentionally sent emails at all hours of the night to impress someone. I have also never been accused of not getting my job done on

Be Yourself—the Paradox

time and I am always cited as doing it with the utmost quality. There is a balance to what I do now. I ensure that I am conscious of my work quality from the beginning and I don't have to panic at the last minute. Work hard. Work smart. Success will take care of itself if you work in the right company and for the right people. If you work in a place where you are constantly on guard, ask yourself, "Is this the right culture for me? Can I be myself?"

63.

Treat Each Day Like an Interview — Another Paradox

In one breath I tell you that you should be yourself; work hard, and things will take care of themselves. In the second breath, I will tell you that every day is an interview. Isn't that contradictory? A good friend of mine, who has years of Human Resource experience, once told me that a job interview is like a first date. You're about to see someone's supposed best and everything he or she has to give. I had an interview recently where the person was a couple minutes late for our discussion. He had no specific reason, and he didn't know a lot about the job. He even mentioned that he was hoping I could tell him about it. He didn't ask for clarity about the role or more details about the job, he wanted me to tell him about the job he applied for. Although some of his answers were decent, and I saw some growth potential, I walked away from what I will describe as an average interview. As much as I wanted to take a chance on him, I also wanted him to put a little more individual effort into what could have been a career-changing moment. If this was his best for our "first date," I should have concerns about what he can do for my team in the future.

The person interviewing, like on a first date, typically will be dressed well (or should be), prepared (or should be), and ready to give you his or her 'A' game. As the person making a hiring decision during an average interview, we sometimes want to justify the candidate's efforts, and hire him anyway. We either have a hiring goal we need to achieve, see something between the lines, or just want to give someone a break. All are legitimate reasons to make a thoughtful decision. As you are making this thoughtful decision, the question needs to be asked of yourself, "You just saw his or her best. Does it go downhill from here?" I have found too many examples of instances when the decision that average was good enough went badly. The person was not a good fit for the company or job. He or she should have given you his or her 'A' game, but we accepted their

Treat Each Day Like an Interview—Another Paradox

'B' or 'C' game, thus setting the expectations and bar lower right off the bat. It may well go downhill from there.

Once you are in the company, the interview process doesn't stop. Your 'A' game shouldn't go away just because you entered the building as an official employee. I know that brand new cars instantly lose their value as soon as you drive it off the lot, but you are not a new car. Your value should grow as you enter the building—every day. Every day you should strive to raise your game. There will be bad days, but you should make an effort to minimize those bad days and strive to add value to the company each day. This includes interactions with people you work with, work for, and the people who work for you. Don't let your guard down and coast for a day. It only starts you down a path of building bad habits.

For example, have you ever been caught off guard when someone started to use profanity because "it's just the two of you." Have you ever been involved in rumor-mill chatter, or bad mouthing a colleague? How about a casual conversation in the hall that turns into a confidential dialogue? You need to realize that you are constantly being watched, listened to, and judged by people at all levels and your reputation is constantly being evaluated.

If someone witnesses your 'B' or 'C' game, it may leave a lasting impression for a while. Every interaction can be viewed as an interview. It doesn't mean you can't have casual or confidential interactions with others; it means be conscious of your actions and words. Every interaction can be a lasting one; make it a good one. Seek to maintain the reputation you want—the reputation that you are making a top notch effort every day. I am also not encouraging you to be uppity, snobbish, or to act better than anyone else out there. I am, however, saying that we should all set an example for others to emulate. Be a role model. Being your natural self should include all of this.

So, is the message to be constantly on guard and never have fun? No. Regardless of whether you are a company leader, an emerging leader, or someone who just wants to be respected in the workplace, you should competently be aware of your surroundings and actions. You should make the effort to be in control of your actions and understand the impression you are leaving on others. This includes being fun. If you create a professional and fun environment where employees work hard and are rewarded for their efforts, people will take notice and respond. They will make their own effort to be professional, want to have fun, and work hard because they see you doing it. If their leaders are doing it, then it must be all right for them.

Be yourself and bring your 'A' game each day; be aware that you are

The Transformation of a Doubting Thomas

a potential role model and you can take the lead to set the tone. You may even get noticed by other decision makers who think you would be a great fit in their shop because they are impressed with you, ironically, for what you may consider an everyday event. Treat each day like an interview—it will pay off.

64.

Be a Teacher — You Will Learn More

I have known many people in the teaching profession who have dedicated their daily lives to teaching children. I often hear how gratifying and rewarding it is to them as individuals. There is also a humbling pride I have witnessed in many school teachers as they watch "their" children grow throughout the school year.

I remember the first time I was asked at school in the fourth grade what I wanted to be when I grew up. Possibly out of panic or the unknown, I said I wanted to be a teacher. Being a school teacher wasn't in my future. I have found I don't have the necessary patience. I have observed teachers—including my wife, who is a teacher by profession—who have shown more patience then I could ever dream of.

I may not have met my fourth grade goal of becoming a teacher, but I have found myself teaching throughout my professional years. I have gone from teaching cold hard facts, to teaching technical aspects of a given job, to investing my time in teaching people how to increase their confidence and improve themselves. I have presented to groups of people, mentored one-on-one, and managed teams of all sizes. I have taught new hires, new managers, tenured employees, and tenured managers over the years. I guess I too have witnessed firsthand the humbling pride of watching others grow.

Watching people learn a new business and better themselves is powerful. However, this feeling of pride is overpowered by the amount of learning I find myself doing whenever I am in teaching mode. I have begun to pick up on the common teachings of patience and humility myself. There are so many things to learn as a teacher of others. I have learned that I could be a better listener and ensure that there are two-way discussions, even in a classroom setting. I have room to improve my style, my delivery, and my preparation. I have learned that I do not know everything, and sharing what I do know is intoxicating. I have learned

The Transformation of a Doubting Thomas

that as a teaching mentor, I can make a difference one person at a time.

I constantly learn from attendees in the classroom setting. I see an eagerness to learn and a thirst to share ideas. I have learned that there is no single best way to do something and that people learn at different speeds. I have learned through the years that people learn in different ways: some like books, some learn visually, and different generations learn differently. I have learned that I need to vary my approach to be more flexible and plan for the unexpected.

One of my biggest lessons is the recognition that I had things to teach. I already knew I had business skills to teach that increased people's technical acumen. However, I found that I had a story to tell, and there were people who wanted to listen. We all have our own background and stories that can be shared. I found that my job satisfaction and success increased when I shared my own lessons learned and best practices.

I found there is an audience to teach. It can be an audience of one or an audience of one hundred. There is an active and willing group of people who are willing to take the steps to be better, learn from one another's wisdom, and get the nuggets of information necessary to strengthen their resolve and confidence—so that they, in turn, can eventually become the teacher. It is a constant and progressive process.

I have found no better learning experience than humbly standing in front of a group of people who want to be there. Whenever possible, seek opportunities in your professional world to be the teacher. Teach someone something—anything—and you will invariably be the student. Your thirst to share will pay off in more knowledge for you to absorb. This ensures a perpetual cycle of teaching and learning.

65.

Value People

When I was in a position to support my business, I was responsible for keeping the day-to-day components running smoothly. I found I had a group of go-to people I constantly needed for assistance. There was one person in particular who worked in technology that I found I was constantly calling to fix something. His sense of urgency and my sense of urgency were quite different. I had the constant need to ride him and follow up to get things done. I would stay on him, and he would quietly get to my requests in his own sweet time.

On one occasion, I really felt that my request needed to be prioritized— although everything seemed urgent to me. He gave me the same response that he gave me every other time: I would wait in line with the other requests and he would get to it. I felt the need to sit down with him this time and explain that I really needed him to get to my request now. We sat together for an extended period for the first time ever. It was not just a quick phone call or email request—we had a real conversation. I explained my reasoning and rationale, which differed from past terse requests, "I need it done now." I hoped in doing this that he would come to understand why my request differed in priority from the other requests he had in his queue. He seemed to understand, and we were able to work out a decent agreement that worked for both of us. I let him know how much I appreciated him jumping on it, and thanked him for the past work he had done for me. I clearly let him know that the work he had done in the past was done with high quality and he should be proud of it. I was not doing this because I just got what I wanted. I was doing this because I felt we finally connected and he deserved to hear it.

Although he was taken aback to begin with, he saw the budding relationship as well and graciously accepted the compliment. He also thought it was a good time to provide me with some honesty of his own. He matter-of-factly said, "You'll catch more flies with honey than vinegar." I had

The Transformation of a Doubting Thomas

heard this proverb before, but never directed specifically at me, but I got the point quickly.

Our relationship continued to grow over time. He continued to increase his sense of urgency, when it made sense, and I started to get more requests done without follow-up. He would move my requests up the queue with a wink, at times. Although this lesson isn't about being someone's favorite, it didn't hurt. In reality, he wasn't working faster, showing more urgency, or even any favoritism, he just wasn't intentionally delaying my requests any longer. I had deserved the delays before because I was not respecting the value of the work he did. It also took an event in which I really needed something badly to force me to tell someone he'd done a great job. Sometimes, people just need to feel valued and appreciated. As a peer or a manager, we should appreciate the whole value of what someone is offering, not just a single event. Don't wait for a particular moment to give a simple compliment and provide recognition.

66.

Revisit the Things That Made You Better and Stronger

Go back and revisit all of the things that inspired you, taught you, and motivated you. Go back and read your collection of leadership books, self-help books, watch your DVDs, or anything else from which you felt you received a strong message that made a difference in your development. Find your old notes from mentor sessions, or interesting technical reading about your industry, or anything that interests you. Dust off old performance appraisals and make sure you have implemented the feedback. What you choose to go back to is not as relevant as reinvesting the time to reinforce past teachings. I personally dedicate at least an hour a week to reference past material and review information I may have forgotten. I'm sure we have all heard the phrase from someone who has been around the block for a while, "I've forgotten more than someone else knows." Don't let that happen to you.

You are a constant evolving, learning creature. Some of the revisited material may seem brand new, while others may simply be viewed from a new and wiser perspective. Keep the learning alive for a better professional and personal future. Most of us are surrounded with learning materials that are right at our fingertips. Be wise and use them.

I have written many times about investing time with mentors and supporters, and surrounding yourself with great teammates. However, only you can take the final step to transform your professional life. I am grateful for everyone who has provided me enough guidance to inspire me to make the choices I have. I believe everyone has a choice to transform their life. I know, because I have. I, the cynic, did not believe in myself—or many others, for that matter—early in my career. The twists and turns of my professional life put me on a path to build my self-confidence and self-awareness. I am the same person, but with a brand new outlook and the confidence that I can make a difference in my life and the

The Transformation of a Doubting Thomas

lives of many others. I can make a difference in my professional career. I can make my business better. I can share my experiences so others can prosper. I have finally learned to take a step back and invest for countless steps forward.

Much of what you have read in this book seems obvious. I like to be the king of the obvious sometimes, because if it was so obvious, then why did it take me so long to grasp hold of much of it? My years of interaction with professionals has proven that we are creatures of habit, and need a little tweaking to find the good habits that make us better. Keep going back to the basics that have proven to work and you can't go wrong. Pick out the ones that work for you. Keep learning from the past and strengthening the future, but stick with the basics.

PART III
Conclusion

What Now?

So I have laid out over twenty years of my professional lessons for you. You now see the many mistakes I have made, and the arduous chore it was to make the vulnerable decision to open up and be willing to learn from them. I have changed for the better. Whether others believe that statement or not isn't important. It is how I feel about myself. I feel that my transformation has made me a better colleague, a better worker, a better leader, a better manager, a better teacher, a better learner, and, more importantly, a better person. I feel less stressed each day that I come into work, because I have the confidence to take it all on. I have my bad days like everyone else. But, I have more good days than bad. I have a confidence level that I have never had before and feel like I have built a network of people who believe in my abilities.

I have to admit that my original thoughts to write this book were just a dream—and not one of those childhood dreams that I always wanted to do. I had just lost a big Toastmasters competition in Canada. I use the word "lost" because it was a competition, but in reality, I won big. I had great enjoyment around the conference portion of that weekend, during which I met many great people, some of whom even thought I was a life coach. I got caught up in telling people how much I had grown over the years. I enthusiastically shared my transformational experiences based on how much I had learned from my mistakes.

I was so impressed with my competitors. I asked the winner, Joey Grondin, if he would be my mentor and help me develop my speeches. He graciously said yes, and we continued to build on our relationship. The next day, I also won a door prize: Joey's book and CD. Call it fate or coincidence that I won a prize that would provide me more confidence. I am not talking about the material items. I am talking about the newly forged relationship that would continue to evolve. As a result of that relationship, I have been given more encouragement to go further than my

What Now?

previous comfort level ever allowed.

I had already been planting the seeds of a book over the past couple of years with many of my speech topics. I had also invested time in mentoring more people and building my own library of teaching materials designed to improve others' communication skills, leadership skills, time management skills, and other professional development needs. The book became a consolidated view of all that I had been trying to share with others. I went for a routine run one day, and simply ran through the door to the computer and put together my outline. The outline turned into a vision and mission, and turned into all the lessons I have learned in my career. Let's revisit both and see where we land.

My vision for writing this book is to provide a simple-to-follow, written guide for professionals hoping to develop their skills in a multitude of areas including communication, leadership, organization, and networking. The lessons are based on my own professional experiences over more than twenty years in a corporate environment. I want to utilize my experiences gained from work, my membership in Toastmasters International (a group of 270,000 world-wide members looking to improve their communication and leadership skills) and the National Speakers Association, and from the epiphanies I have experienced by teaching a professional development series. In addition to my normal job responsibilities, I started investing time with emerging leaders and experienced managers a couple years ago in an attempt to teach my lessons to others. I want to spread those teachings to a broader audience.

My mission is to create an easy-to-read guide that will motivate and inspire you to take the steps to transform yourself. I want you to improve your professional experiences and increase the positive impacts you have on the people around you. Whether you are working in a small business or a large corporation, you will be able to apply these examples and teachings to your situation. Whether you are a manager, an entry-level employee just joining a company, someone struggling to get through the daily grind, or a professional striving to reach the heights of your career, there will be something in here for you. The book will navigate through key teaching moments from my professional life and offer you a simple reference guide for better organizing your professional life and effectively maneuvering through the complexities of communication, relationship building, and organization.

I set out to teach you the wisdom left on my doorstep either through self-awareness (over long periods of time in some cases) or through shared lessons from people I now emulate. I intentionally wrote "now"

The Transformation of a Doubting Thomas

since I had thought cynically of many of them in the past or did not respect them as I do now. Even in situations when there was a barrier I could not break through with someone, whether it was due to different styles or personality clashes, I have looked back and learned something from that situation in my professional career.

My cynicism held me back. The concepts in this book are so simple in nature, yet were so complex to add to my everyday thinking and everyday belief system. I know that I am no rocket scientist, but I am a proud employee of twenty plus years. Hard work has not paid off as much as smart work. I am so appreciative of the people who have touched my professional life, including the individuals bold enough to stare me in the face and say I needed to improve. That includes the person in the mirror who became strong enough to say, "It's time for a change. It's time to make a difference for myself and others. It's time to transform."

The list of my lessons is not all-inclusive because I don't know where it is going to end. Learning is a constant process and should never cease. I was convinced I would never need to take another class after I left college. In a conversation during one of my rotational mentor programs, I was told that my thirst for knowledge could take me to my MBA and beyond. I was being pushed to take the next step in my education. I spent several days thinking about my response to him. I came back and said, "Thanks, but no thanks." My response was not because I wouldn't gain from additional scholastics, but I felt I would sacrifice putting my heart and soul into learning as much as possible of the business I had sitting in front of me. I had an entire ocean of learning and I was only at the shore about to dive in. The concept of transforming me further was starting to gain momentum at this time, and I still feel I made the right decision, for now. I am not done because I am far from perfect, but I am excited for the road ahead. I have grown from a cynic to someone thirsty for what comes next.

I have found a long career with the majority of it with same company to be a great reward. Whether you have had the same job, worked with the same company, or moved around regularly, you are doing it to find the right moves for you. Even if a decision was made for you, I am a firm believer that things happen for a reason. The reason is usually dictated by the fact that you have done the right things leading up to it, whether it is through your own preparation or meeting the right people.

I had an uncle who worked for a company in system technology for many years. Besides being an extremely loyal person, he was a nice guy. The economy caused his job to be eliminated. He graciously went out without stepping on any toes, and actually took calls from his previous

What Now?

colleagues on "how to do more with less" for jobs in which his old peers had no expertise. He had lain the groundwork years before with his leadership and job knowledge. He knew patience and timing would eventually pay off. They did. He was offered his old job back because they couldn't do it without him. However, the nice guy took some cues from the "you not only want me" mentality; he went down the "you really need me" path and asked for more than he originally had. It was a fair assessment and he knew he did not need to roll over. He learned a little about himself and the corporate world during his time off and deserved everything on top of what he'd had when he left.

I also had a friend who was caught up in job cuts. He was told he needed to either find a position he was qualified for in a department where there were openings within the company, or he would lose his existing job within forty-five days. He had the support of friends and colleagues convinced he was good for the company. Together, the whole network was on the move to ultimately find him something that ended up being a position where he had greater responsibility. It is funny how things work out with a little effort and a great support system. Although we all have 20/20 hindsight about mistakes made in the past, we still have luxury of looking forward to the next challenge of the unknown that may have previously caused fear.

Personality, emotion, politics, and corporate culture may get in the way of our transformation, but we can eventually get there. Regardless of your generation, experience, or current position, you are in a position to become better and stronger. The vision and mission were to provide you with some tangible examples and lessons to strengthen yourself in a way that was easy to grasp. I have had my vision clouded in the past, but feel the importance of this mission to move it forward. When I ask, "What now?" I am asking myself and you. I'm sure I have plenty of new lessons I could toss into a new book, but the path has yet to be shown. I will continue to teach, and more importantly, learn.

I will be impatiently patient in driving my performance, my growth, and my lessons learned. I even have to ensure I take my own advice. In 2010, I was tapped on the shoulder as a potential candidate in a business that I had never been in before. I was excited to learn a new business. I was pulled in two directions, since I had been in my current role for less than nine months. I loved what I was doing. I loved my boss, and I found myself fascinated by the dynamic nature of the current business.

I went through the interviews quickly because there seemed to be an urgency placed on the requests. Yet, after those interviews, which I personally thought had gone well, the communications went silent. It

The Transformation of a Doubting Thomas

did not make sense. Although putting my name in the ring was a well-thought-out decision that included discussions with my family about the potential impact to my hours (most likely having to work West Coast hours while on the East Coast), there was still some excitement attached to the potential of fulfilling a goal when it came to the level of responsibilities I would have taken on.

The extra time allowed me to rethink my decision. I had to repeat to myself: I loved what I was doing. I loved my boss, and I found myself fascinated by the dynamic nature of the current business. I had just answered my own question. Although I felt surrounded by great people in the current role, they had made it clear that they would never hold me back from growing. This felt good to hear. They had my back and had even offered to make calls on my behalf to get me the new position. I felt that I would be cutting my learning curve short if I left at that point. I decided to stay for selfish reasons, because I was surrounded with a cast of people dedicated to becoming leaders in the industry, all of whom were seeing the bigger picture. I wanted to be a part of that vision. I was willing to take my chances to grow and be a little more patient. This one was a clear decision in staying to do what I love while allowing myself to continue to be challenged. Ironically, in a "Wait three month" sort of way, I was offered an expanded role that I couldn't refuse shortly after that decision. It was in a field in which I was an expert, it was a start-up operation, and I could build my own organization. I left my old team behind with a sense of loyalty and pride, knowing that they were there for me, and I approached the new job with fervor for making a difference in the overall organization. I saw a bright future in my new role, in which I could use my strengths and play off my past lessons.

I now have an inside-out view of my future. I have spent too much time in my past pushing people away and blaming the powers that be for my failures. The internalization of assessing my own failures is enlightening. I have become addicted to making myself better, and have taken to asking advice of anyone willing to hear the question, "What can I do to make myself better?" I am dependent on co-workers, family, friends, mentors, Toastmasters, strangers (rotational mentors), and people who work for and with me to provide critical feedback that I am responsible for integrating into my growth. I am the proud owner of feedback and carefully have to take the actions necessary to truly benefit from it.

You have just taken part in the journey of who I am professionally. I get the luxury of the therapy attached to draining all of my thoughts, opinions, stories, and lessons learned onto the blank page. Many of my frustrations bubbled up after years of repressed memories, while others flooded

What Now?

out way too quickly. I hope the common sense aspect hits home—though I know that "Hope won't win the game without a game plan. Take action." My action plan is the book. It is my guide to reinforcing what I need to practice each day. I am not a shoot-to-the-top employee. I am a loyal, dedicated senior leader of a company, who is confident enough to say I have earned everything I have gotten, and earned everything I didn't get.

The experience in organizing the many random thoughts that have filled my mind for years was a lesson itself in ensuring I believed what I was saying. The experience will have a lasting impact in understanding whether I can effectively influence and persuade just one person to take action. I already have, because *I* am moving forward more effectively than before. I am appreciative of everyone who helped me through my personal and professional life to realize I have not peaked yet and my potential is still waiting to be fulfilled.

Cynicism is contagious, if you allow it. So is inspiration and motivation. I had two roads to look down, and I chose the path of transformation. I am not a life coach, nor do I want to pretend to be one. I am someone who has passion burning in me that needed to be released in a targeted fashion that would do well for my own self-motivated reasons, while at the same time being good for any business and people within an organization. I am the former, or recovering, "Doubting Thomas" who now believes in the ability of people to transform their negativity to something positive. I am humbled to admit my mistakes and willing to shout what I have learned from the rooftops. I still haven't answered the question, "What now?" What I want to do now is be better today than I was yesterday, and continue to make the transformation toward someone I want to be. When I am done, I'm going to do it all over again.

References

Branham, Leigh. *The 7 Hidden Reasons Employees Leave.* New York: Amacon, 2005.

Buxton, Ryan. Study: "Multitasking May Be Detrimental to Information Retention." Isureveille.com. September 7, 2009.

Carlson, Richard, PH.D. *Don't Sweat the Small Stuff...and it's all small stuff.* New York: Hyperion, 1997.

Collins, James C., and Jerry I. Porras. *Built to Last: Successful Habits of Visionary Companies.* New York: HarperBusiness, 1994.

Covey, Steven R. *The 7 Habits of Highly Effective People: Powerful Lessons in Personal Change.* New York: Simon & Schuster, 1989.

Grondin, Joseph. *Living in Harmony With Our Children.* First Choice Books, 2010.

Giuliani, Rudolph W. *Leadership.* New York: Hyperion, 2002.

Hersey, Dr. Paul. *The Situational Leader.* Escondido, CA: The Center for Leadership Studies, Inc., 1984.

Kaye, Beverly and Sharon Jordan-Evans. *Love 'Em or Lose 'Em: Getting Good People to Stay.* San Francisco: Berrett-Koehler Publishers, Inc., 2005.

Tolstoy, Leo. *War and Peace.* New York: Random House, 1869.

References

Watkins, Michael. *The First 90 Days: Critical Success Strategies for New Leaders at All Levels.* Harvard Business Press, 2003.
Winget, Larry. *It's Called Work for a Reason: Your Success is Your Own Damn Fault.* New York: Gotham Books, 2007.

Uzzi, Brian and Shannon Dunlap. *How to Build Your Network.* Harvard Business Review, December 2005. www.hbr.org.

Acknowledgements

I want to thank all of the people I have crossed paths with over my entire professional career, including the summer jobs I had growing up. The people I worked with, worked for, and customers I served all had a significant impact on who I am today, both personally and professionally—whether I like it or not. There are some who drove me down the path of cynicism, and there are those who saved me from my own negativity. I had a saying that morphed over time as I moved through a company or had teammates change responsibilities, which I referenced in the Mentor chapter: "Don't step on any toes, don't burn any bridges, and keep the lines of communications open." The balance of the message between communication, networking, and always looking for the positive in everyone has stood the test of time as I have continued to reference it.

There are far too many people whose paths I have crossed to name individually. However, there are leaders, mentors, friends, and family who have been there to support me as I was going through my own growing pains and searching to find who I wanted to be as a leader in the complex corporate world. In addition to the incredible assistance in understanding the book business from Tris Coburn, I want to thank Steve Crawford, Jeff Schmidt, Neal Williamson, Chip Rossi, Bob Shiflet, Jeff Nathan, Kathy Bernath, Kathleen Fitzgerald, Erin Dymowski, Steve Dymowski and Vin Contento for falling into multiple categories as leaders, mentors, and friends.

I want to also thank Cynthia Martin, Kim Mitchell, Polly Hall, Paula Williamson, and Carmen Felix, who invested the time to read through the first rough drafts of the book and offer their candid feedback to build up the messages I wanted to convey. I want to thank my editor, Jen Blood, from Maine Authors Publishing for strengthening my work.

From the onset, Dirigo Toastmasters—my local club—has been instrumental in encouraging me through speech competitions and

Acknowledgements

pushing me to improve my communication skills. My Toastmasters contacts have grown through networking, competitions, and conferences. Each of them has left a mark as I have molded my style. I want to personally thank Joey Grondin for showing me how to refine my style and maximize the potential I had in writing and delivering winning speeches.

I want to also thank my incredible wife, Ellen, who told me the things I didn't think I wanted or needed to hear to make me a better husband, father, friend, communicator, and leader. She has been behind the project since the beginning, when I surprised her with the idea out of the blue. The great thing is that she is no longer surprised by my surprises, since she wasn't expecting my marriage proposal either. My three children Meg, Erin, and Tatum have also been instrumental in teaching me that life is too precious to waste with cynicism. They too have become active in pushing me further to reach my potential in everything I do.

About the Author

Tom Dowd finished his last day of college on a Friday and started his professional business career the following Monday. He graduated from the University of Delaware in 1990 with a Communication degree, concentrating on interpersonal and organizational communication. Tom has over twenty years of experience in the corporate world in management and leadership roles. He had to proactively learn how to maneuver through the complexities and diverse dynamics of the corporate world if he wanted to survive enough to make a difference and be successful. Tom joined Toastmasters International in 2008, where he quickly gained success as an award-winning speaker and leader. He was selected as the 2010-11 District 45 Toastmaster of the Year and is also a member of the National Speakers Association. In 2011 his expertise as a speaker, author, trainer, and coach led him to start his own business, *Thomas Dowd Professional Development & Coaching*. Tom frequently presents to, and coaches, a wide variety of audiences ranging from students, community members, and professionals. He can be reached through his website at www.transformationtom.com. In addition to this book, he is simultaneously publishing *From Fear to Success: A Practical Public-speaking Guide*.

Tom lives in Camden, Maine with his wife and three daughters.